GOLD RUSH DOGS

Claire Rudolf Murphy & Jane G. Haigh

Hillside Press

For Molly, whose love of dogs inspired this book.—J. G. H.

To Pat, Margarita, and Stefka Kling, and their beloved dog, Buddy.—C. R. M.

Yukon quartet.

Text © 2001 and 2012 by Claire Rudolf Murphy &
Jane G. Haigh

Originally published by Alaska Northwest Books®, Portland,
Oregon, 2001

Second edition published by Hillside Press, 2012
Second printing, 2015

Library of Congress Control Number: 2012905318

ISBN: 978-0-9627530-6-0

Hillside Press
1222 Well Street, Suite 3
Fairbanks, AK 99701
www.janehaigh.com

Design: Elizabeth Watson
Maps: Gray Mouse Graphics
Production: Susan Dupèré

Photographs: The photos in this book are from numerous
institutional and private collections. Photo credits are listed
on page 116.
Front cover: Center—Julian; Left, top to bottom—Togo, Nero,
Baldy of Nome, Patsy Ann. *Back cover:* Canine papoose.

Printed in China

Canine papoose.

He who gives time to the study

of the history of Alaska, learns that the dog,

next to man, has been the most important factor

in its past and present development.

—Alaska Judge James Wickersham, in 1938

CONTENTS

Dog buddies.

"Murphy" with his well-equipped pack sacks may be the most popular dog photo from the Klondike era. This photo shows up under different names in many different collections.

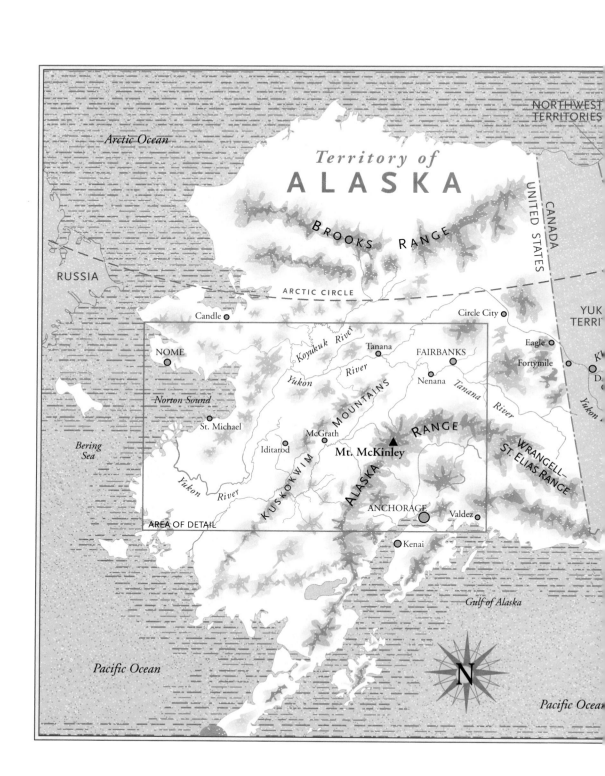

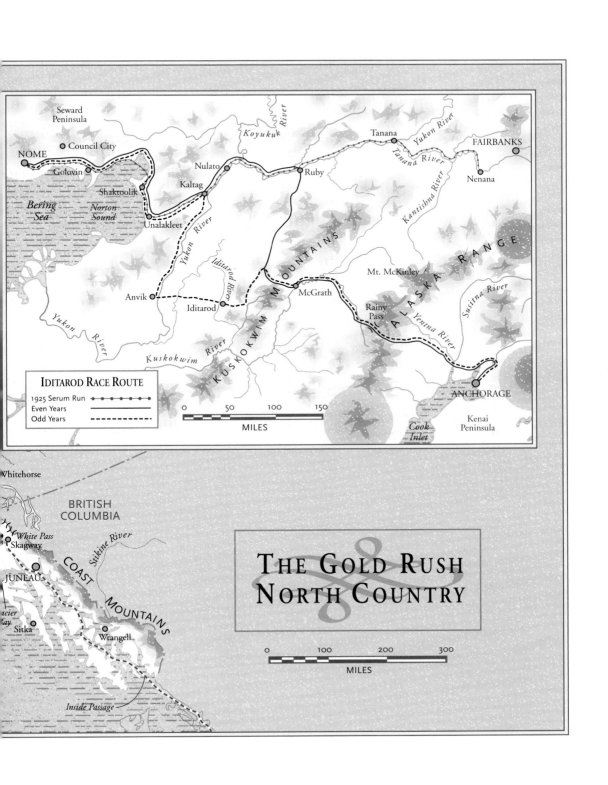

Seward
Peninsula

Koyukuk River

Tanana

Yukon River

FAIRBANKS

NOME

Council City

Golovin

Nulato

Tanana River

Ruby

Nenana

Kaltag

Shaktoolik

*Bering
Sea*

*Norton
Sound*

Unalakleet

Yukon River

Kantishna River

Iditarod River

KUSKOKWIM MOUNTAINS

Mt. McKinley

A L A S K A   R A N G E

Anvik

McGrath

Susitna River

Iditarod

Rainy
Pass

Yentna River

Yukon River

Kuskokwim River

ANCHORAGE

Kenai
Peninsula

*Cook
Inlet*

IDITAROD RACE ROUTE

1925 Serum Run	●—●—●—●—●
Even Years	——
Odd Years	– – –

0   50   100   150

MILES

Whitehorse

BRITISH
COLUMBIA

Stikine River

White Pass

Skagway

JUNEAU

COAST MOUNTAINS

Sitka

...cier
...ay

Wrangell

Inside Passage

THE GOLD RUSH
NORTH COUNTRY

0   100   200   300

MILES

INTRODUCTION
THE INDISPENSABLE DOG
OF THE NORTHLAND

*In every part of the world, the dog is the companion
and helper of man, but nowhere is he so essentially a part of the life
of the people as in the northern part of this continent.*

—Tappan Adney, *Harper's Weekly* correspondent, 1899

Legions of treasure seekers during the Alaska-Yukon gold rush era depended on the loyalty and hard work of their dogs. Revered as companions and as partners in labor, the animals were treated by many prospectors and other citizens of gold country as beloved members of the family. The dogs often left a legacy of devotion, even heroism. *Gold Rush Dogs* tells the stories of some of the most remarkable of these animals.

Like domesticated dogs everywhere, gold rush dogs were faithful, enthusiastic comrades—the best antidote to cabin fever during the endless Northern winters. But there was an added dimension to many of these animals: they were workers. Pulling sleds through the snow, they hauled supplies to the mines, transported people, and

◄◄◄ *Alice Hagar, with her baby strapped to her back, uses pack dogs to carry supplies in the Yukon Territory, circa 1930.*

◄◄ *Crowds gathered in the streets of Nome to watch the start of the big races, circa 1913.*

▲ *Three young Eskimo girls dressed in traditional cloth parkas hold their favorite puppies.*

In an era consumed with greed, [the dogs] were sometimes the only ones a lonely gold seeker could trust. They were packhorse, transit system, security guard, and pal rolled into one. They were truly worth their weight in gold.

moved the mail. And in an era consumed with greed, they were sometimes the only ones a lonely gold seeker could trust. They were packhorse, transit system, security guard, and pal rolled into one. They were truly worth their weight in gold.

Gold rush dogs represented a spirit, not a breed. Some were the huskies or malamutes of Alaska tradition. But they also included the mastiff Julian, hauling record loads to the goldfields; the Tahltan bear dog Stickeen, racing John Muir across the glaciers; and the mixed-breed "one-man dog" known as Yukon, protecting his master in a boomtown full of desperadoes. They differed in outward appearance, but not in heart. Bull terrier or mastiff, spaniel or St. Bernard, these dogs shared an endless energy, intelligence, and determination.

Dogs have been important players in the drama of the Far North for thousands of years. Indians and Eskimos bred dogs and relied on them for transportation and load carrying. The Athabascan Indians of the Interior used dogs to pull sleds bearing household goods as they moved to seasonal hunting, fishing, and trapping grounds. For hunting, they sometimes used dogs to pull toboggans made of birch. In summer, the animals might carry packsaddles. The Yup'ik and Inupiat Eskimos on the coast used heavy dogsleds of driftwood, with bone runners. Dogs were secured with a clever harness made of a single piece of bearskin with three slits. Modern dog-mushing equipment and techniques developed over time from these beginnings.

The Klondike gold strike of 1896 brought a stampede of treasure seekers, and dogs became a precious resource amid this frantic scene. The stampeders urgently needed the animals for hauling gear and supplies. A dog that sold for fifteen dollars in Washington State could bring ten times that in the Yukon.

Many of these dogs became as famous as their celebrated owners, or even more so. Nero, the St. Bernard owned by Belinda Mulrooney, richest woman in the Klondike, was known to all on the streets of Dawson City. The mastiff Julian, who helped Klondike stampeder Clarence Berry become a millionaire, was

described in his very own obituary in a San Francisco newspaper as the "most famous dog in Alaska."

Dogs and dog drivers became especially important in Nome, a gold rush community totally isolated for the nine months of winter. To test their boasts about who had the fastest dogs and to create excitement for the gambling crowd, Nome invented the modern sport of long-distance sled-dog racing. The elaborate rules of the Nome Kennel Club written in 1908 still serve as the basis of the sport today. Baldy and Togo were two dogs famed for their racing prowess, but they are remembered even more for going to the aid of humans in distress. Baldy ran to the rescue of his injured musher, and Togo led the toughest leg of the dogsled relay in 1925 that brought lifesaving diphtheria serum to Nome. Another hero of the serum run, the scrappy little freight dog Balto, led the final team into Nome and won the lion's share of public acclaim.

An Athabascan man from the McKenzie River has his large huskies hitched to a birch toboggan.

The dogs of the North inspired a great deal of writing, both fact and fiction. People in Alaska and the Yukon could recognize their own dogs in the heroes of Jack London's stories. Both Nero and Julian were often cited as models for Buck, the hero of London's *The Call of the Wild.* The real-life dog Yukon warned Skagway Bill of danger from outlaws, while Jack London's make-believe White Fang saved his master's family from a marauder. The actual Baldy rushed to help musher Scotty Allan, while the fictional Yukon King of radio and TV fame was always ready to aid Sergeant Preston. Baldy lives on in the pages of Esther Birdsall Darling's *Baldy of Nome;* the little glacier traveler Stickeen is forever remembered because of John Muir's memorable story about him.

Heroes or not, dogs figure in nearly every account of life in Alaska and the Yukon during the late 1800s and early 1900s. The stories are often told in the most personal of terms, relating each dog's personality and special manner. Missionary Hudson Stuck, who mushed many miles in those days, says that it was "a pleasure to come back to Nanook after any long absence. . . ." John Muir says of Stickeen: "He had sensitive ears and sharp eyes. A queer character, odd, concealed, independent, keeping invincibly quiet, and doing many puzzling things."

Baldy of Nome at the starting post of the sixth All Alaska Sweepstakes race in Nome, 1913.

The diphtheria serum run to Nome highlighted the critical importance of sled dogs in the life of the North. But as the gold rush era came to an end, airplanes and snow machines began replacing dog teams as the most practical forms of transport. A new dramatic hero, the bush pilot, took the place of the brave dog musher and the high-spirited sled dog in the popular imagination.

The dogs of today rarely haul mail, or freight to the mines, or lifesaving medicine to isolated villages—but many of them are working as enthusiastically as ever, pulling sleds in thousand-mile races. As the partners of modern mushers in such races as the Iditarod and the Yukon Quest, the dogs of the North have regained much of their former gold rush glory. And through the long days of summer and the short, dark days of winter, they continue to offer companionship and comfort.

Children in front of the one-room Garden Island School, on the outskirts of Fairbanks, prepare for a winter outing with dogsleds and snowshoes, circa 1910.

Fort Wrangel Alaska

Chapter 1

STICKEEN
GLACIER EXPLORER

The icy blue of the glacier seemed to stretch out forever in the white fog of a sudden snow squall. Stickeen pranced around the knees of naturalist John Muir, who was dressed in a long tweed coat. Muir's reddish hair flowed from beneath his Scottish cap. The year was 1880, and on this particular morning, Muir and the little black dog that followed him everywhere had left the other members of their party at a beach camp. The two set out to explore the glacier at the head of Taylor Inlet, southwest of Glacier Bay in Southeast Alaska.

Climbing onto the glacier, dog and man crossed its surface for three miles to reach the other side, then wandered north. By evening, after a long day of exploration, Stickeen and Muir found themselves far from camp. The light fading, they headed back toward the bay, picking their way across the glacier. As they tried to hurry along, they confronted crevasse after crevasse—fearful cracks in the ice that created narrow canyons, disappearing deep into the bowels of the glacier.

The two companions had been able to leap across each of these obstacles. But suddenly their way was blocked by the deepest, most forbidding crevasse of all—one that was far too wide to jump over.

◄ ◄ ◄ *A group of late-nineteenth-century tourists pose on the Muir Glacier as their ship waits offshore, circa 1885.*

◄ ◄ *Stikine Tlingit Indians pose in front of a tribal house with totem poles in Wrangell, 1889.*

▲ *Stickeen was a Tahltan bear dog, a dog indigenous to the mountainous interior of British Columbia and the Yukon.*

Stickeen and Muir walked for miles up and back at the edge of the crevasse, seeking some safe route around or over the chasm. There was none, and in the end they had to settle for a tenuously thin, knife-edged ice bridge that spanned the deadly gulf. Muir must have been afraid, but perhaps more out of concern for Stickeen than for himself. Muir could probably maneuver across this delicate bridge. But could Stickeen?

It was only that year that Muir had joined forces with the dog, who had been acquired as a puppy by the Rev. S. Hall Young and his wife, missionaries to the Stikine Indians, a Tlingit tribe from Wrangell. When tribal leaders came for their first solemn social call on the Youngs, their attention was distracted by the dog. To the Youngs, the puppy was just a black bunch of curly fur with a persistent bark. But the Tlingits recognized him as a rare Tahltan bear dog from Interior Alaska, prized as a species for hunting bears and other game and thus conferring prestige on its owner. The Natives asked that the dog be named for the tribe, thus bringing it under their protection.

"Stickeen grew in beauty," Young later wrote, "if not greatly in stature. His glossy, long, silky hair hung in wavy luxuriance almost to the ground—black with irregular white and tan spots. A magnificent heavily fringed tail curling nearly to his ears wagged on forever. Those silly ears—only less expressive than his tail—rose and fell with every shade of his emotions. He was full of mischief and play, the life of the mission."

When John Muir arrived in Southeast Alaska in 1880 to continue the glacier explorations he had started the year before, Young handled the arrangements for his visit, securing Tlingit guides and a twenty-five-foot cedar canoe loaded with supplies. At the last minute, Stickeen jumped in the canoe to join the trip.

"I liked dogs, but this one seemed so small and dull and worthless," Muir said later. He suggested that Stickeen stay home and play with the children, telling Young: "This trip is not one for toy dogs." But Young confidently assured Muir that, however silly Stickeen might appear, he could "endure cold and hunger like a

But Young confidently assured Muir that, however silly Stickeen might appear, he could "endure cold and hunger like a polar bear, was a capital sailor, and could swim like a seal."

On October 18, 1867, at Russia's Alaskan capital of Sitka, the Russian flag was lowered and the American flag was raised. Most Americans looked on their new territory as worthless. Even those more knowledgeable believed that Alaska was valuable only for its seals, sea otters, and abundance of fish, which had sustained and enriched the Russian-America Company. The gold rush days were still years in the future.

United States ownership of Alaska eventually brought American missionaries to the territory, including Presbyterian minister S. Hall Young, the owner of John Muir's glacier companion Stickeen. Young was sent to Wrangell, where the Stikine Tlingit tribe had settled, and where the house of Chief Shakes dominated the small boat harbor, as it still does today. It was through Wrangell that many prospectors made their way to the 1871 Cassiar gold strike in British Columbia.

The little dog Stickeen always leaped at the chance for another adventure with naturalist John Muir.

In 1880, Joe Juneau and Richard Harris discovered gold in Silver Bow Basin, and the town that grew up there took Juneau's name. Soon the prospectors in Juneau began to pursue the rumors of greater strikes in the Interior of Alaska along the creeks and tributaries of the Yukon River. In 1892 gold was discovered near Forty Mile; in 1894 at Circle City; and then in 1896 in the neighboring Yukon Territory of Canada, on a tributary of the Throndiuk River.

The name Throndiuk, or *tron-diuck,* is an Athabascan word meaning "hammered water." It refers to the wooden stakes that Athabascans hammered into the bed of the river to anchor nets and weirs for catching fish. But many people pronounced the river's name as Klondike—a name that soon came to represent an entire region and is forever associated with one of the world's great gold rushes.

polar bear, was a capital sailor, and could swim like a seal." So Stickeen accompanied the expedition.

For two weeks they paddled north, making camp on rocky beaches that separated the sea from dense northern rain forest and towering mountains. Each time the party got ready to paddle away from a campsite, Stickeen would disappear into the woods to hunt squirrels. No matter how the men called and cajoled, Stickeen would wait until they pushed off from shore, then suddenly appear

Naturalist John Muir was a relatively young man in 1880 when he made his famous trip with Stickeen.

Born in Scotland in 1838, John Muir grew up in Wisconsin but lived most of his life in California. He was founder of the Sierra Club, which grew into one of the great environmental organizations of the United States. When Muir arrived in Wrangell in 1879 on the first of his seven trips to Alaska, he had already made a name for himself by exploring and describing the valleys of Yosemite and the Sierra Nevada. He was among the first to attribute the dramatic rock formations of Yosemite Valley to the work of ancient glaciers, and it was with much excitement that he set off to explore the living glaciers of Southeast Alaska.

Muir usually embarked alone onto these heavily crevassed oceans of ice, without the modern safeguards of crampons, rope, or companions. Often his only food consisted of the hard-tack crackers he carried in the pockets of his long tweed coat. Upon surviving another such trek, he would speak enthusiastically of the wonders he had seen.

"I've been a thousand feet down in the crevasses, with matchless domes and sculptured figures and carved ice-work all about me," he wrote. "Solomon's marble and ivory palaces were nothing to it. Such purity, such color, such delicate beauty! I was tempted to stay there and feast my soul, and softly freeze, until I would become part of the glacier. What a great death that would be!"

For many years, Muir told the story of Stickeen in order to engage listeners in descriptions of his glacier travels. From 1879 to 1882, Muir published forty-one articles in the *San Francisco Bulletin,* feeding the public's insatiable curiosity about "Seward's ice box"— the Alaska territory that the United States, under Secretary of State William Henry Seward, bought from Russia in 1867.

Muir's writings and enthusiasm about Alaska gave rise to a wave of travel to the Northland. In 1883, the first of many tourist ships cruised into Glacier Bay, where an immense glacier was named in Muir's honor. He died in 1914, just before publication of his famous book, *Travels to Alaska,* a compilation of his magazine articles.

and paddle out to the canoe as if this was his favorite part of the trip. Muir would dredge the little dog out of the water, holding him out for a moment and shaking him dry. Once safely back aboard, Stickeen would make himself at home, curling up in the bottom with the baggage.

Eager to explore, Stickeen followed Muir everywhere and proved himself to be a calm, nearly fearless companion. Thus it was that they found themselves on the glacier that fateful day, confronting the challenge of crossing a huge crevasse.

With darkness falling and many miles remaining to camp, Muir realized they would have to cross the thin sliver of ice that spanned the chasm. To reach this bridge, Muir carefully carved steps for five feet down the wall of the crevasse. There he turned and sat astride the bridge, one leg dangling down each side. Slowly he eased across, scooting gingerly over to the other wall. He now cut more steps to get up the cliff and back onto the surface of the glacier. Then he turned and waited for Stickeen to follow.

Stickeen at the heels of his master, John Muir.

Stickeen, who had been so willing, so fearless up to now, was frantic. He wailed and whined, as if to say, "I can never go down there!" Muir talked to the dog, as he would to a child. "Hush your fears, my boy," Muir murmured softly. "We will get safely across, though it will not be easy."

Stickeen only whined again, and ran back and forth looking for a way out.

"You can come if you will only try, Stickeen," Muir pleaded.

In desperation, Muir hid behind a mound of ice, trying to fool Stickeen into believing he had gone on. Perhaps then the dog would follow. But Stickeen only laid down and moaned. Muir gave up the game and came out again to the brink of the abyss.

"Come on, boy, you can make it if you try!" he shouted across the crevasse.

Then Muir became stern: "I must certainly leave you, Stickeen. I can wait no longer. It will soon be dark, and if you go back to the woods the wolves will certainly eat you."

Finally the desperate little dog seemed to swallow his fear. He

Stikeen knew his
only chance lay in
crossing the
fearsome crevasse.

crouched on the brink of the crevasse and pressed his body against the ice, then slid his paws down to the first step. Slowly he slithered down the steps to the bridge. Then he walked with careful determination over the narrow span that would bring him back to Muir.

Finally at the other side, he paused, but before Muir could reach down to him, Stickeen sprang up the steps to safety. Yelping for joy, he darted and swirled in giddy loops, rolled over twice, and turned head over heels, all the while emitting a series of sobs.

They still had a long way to go, across the glacier and through the forest. It was with great relief that they finally reached camp, where they enjoyed the campfire and a big supper. But through the

Stickeen—with his short legs and compact body, his long, silky hair and bushy, foxlike tail—was a typical Tahltan bear dog. A rare breed, these little animals were one of the few aboriginal dogs of North America.

The Tahltan bear dog was commemorated in this 1988 Canadian stamp as one of the few dogs indigenous to Canada.

The dogs were native to the mountainous interior of northeast British Columbia and southern Yukon Territory, where they were domesticated by the inland Tlingit, Casca, Sikanni, and Tahltan Indians. The Tahltans called them "our dogs," and so they were named.

Black or black and tan in color, these dogs stood only twelve to sixteen inches high and weighed ten to eighteen pounds. Natives hunted with the little dogs that, unlike the larger malamutes and huskies, were especially well fed and cared for, often sleeping in the tent with the family.

Unlikely as it seems, the Tahltans were particularly suited for hunting bears. With their incessant barking and nimble darting attacks, they could harass a bear to a baffled standstill. Hunters sometimes carried them in backpacks to conserve the dogs' strength.

"They were very smart dogs," said John Carlick, a Tahltan elder. "They could find a bear's den through the deep snow. They could chase up grouse and ptarmigan. They could find rabbits, anything. If you had a bear dog, you could find game; if you didn't have a bear dog, you starved."

After 1906 the numbers of these dogs dwindled, perhaps through interbreeding. In spite of some efforts to keep the breed alive, the Tahltan bear dog finally disappeared.

night, even though he fell into an exhausted sleep, Stickeen kept springing up and whimpering, as if dreaming that he was still on the brink of the crevasse.

Muir returned home to California and later wrote about his day on the glacier with Stickeen. Although that hazardous outing took place nearly twenty years before the big Northern gold strikes, the story wasn't published until the time of the great Klondike rush. The tale has now taken its place alongside the stories of other memorable dogs of the North.

After his close escape from the glacier, Stickeen became a favorite pet at the mission in Wrangell. Then one summer day in 1883, Stickeen could not be found. The Rev. and Mrs. Young feared that the charming dog had been enticed on board the monthly supply ship that had just pulled out of Wrangell. The fate of this brave, intense little dog forever remained a mystery.

Then one summer day in 1883, Stickeen could not be found. . . . The fate of this brave, intense little dog forever remained a mystery.

Chapter 2

JULIAN

MIGHTY MASTIFF

In the spring of 1896, Clarence J. Berry and his party made camp at the bottom of the fearsomely steep route to Chilkoot Pass. Then he and his dog team, led by a two-hundred-pound yellow mastiff named Julian, ferried load after load to the top. The Chilkoot Trail, which took miners from near Skagway, Alaska, into the Yukon, was less a trail than an ordeal. Starting along the beach at Dyea, Alaska, and then following the Dyea River, the route climbed over the treacherous pass and continued on to Canada's Lake Bennett.

After the grueling uphill travel, the flat terrain of Lake Bennett looked easy. But instead, the rough ice and strong winds presented even more challenges for the sled dogs. At this point, the other dogs in Berry's team were nearly worn out. So Julian pulled the entire sled load of more than a thousand pounds across the frozen lake by himself. With remarkable feats like this, Julian eventually became the best-known dog in the goldfields of Alaska and the Yukon.

Clarence J. Berry—better known as "CJ"—returned from his first trip to the Yukon in 1895 and came back realizing the value of dogs for transporting people and goods. He returned to California to marry his twenty-three-year-old fiancée, Ethel Bush—and to train a team of sled dogs for work in the North. CJ bought Julian

◄◄◄ *Fred Berry, second from left, and his workers pose with Julian in front of the Berry cabin on their Eldorado Creek claim in 1898.*

◄◄ *An honored member of the Berry family, Julian posed for a formal studio portrait with Fred Berry and Mrs. "Tot" Berry's dog, Precious.*

▲ *Julian, a yellow mastiff from California, proved his worth in the Klondike.*

29

THE KLONDIKE GOLD RUSH

Claim owners still lived in tents on their claims on Bonanza Creek, site of the gold discovery that started the Klondike gold rush, when this photo was taken circa 1898–99.

George Carmack appeared in Bill McPhee's saloon in Forty Mile in August 1896 with a shotgun shell full of gold flakes. He announced to the crowd that he had discovered gold on Rabbit Creek, a tributary of the river the Indians called the Throndiuk—and that miners called the Klondike. Carmack did not have the reputation of being a serious prospector, and few of the experienced miners believed him. But eager newcomers like Clarence Berry rushed off to stake their claims.

These claims on creeks that were renamed Bonanza and Eldorado turned out to be the big strike that miners on the Yukon had dreamed of and sought for more than twenty years. To get to their treasure, the Klondike miners had to sink shafts through frozen ground. Gold that was washed down by ancient streams had been deposited on the bedrock fifteen, twenty, even forty feet below the surface.

While the miners washed out rich pans of gold from the bottom of their shafts, the world remained largely ignorant of the new strike. The miners—and word of their discoveries—were locked into the icy

Interior and would not get out until spring. Then, when the first riverboat steamed up the Yukon, they boarded it for the long ride down the river to St. Michael on the Bering Sea, where they boarded the steamers *Excelsior* and *Portland,* bound for the West Coast of the United States.

The world learned of the new goldfields in July 1897 when the ragged miners clambered down the gangplank of the *Excelsior* in San Francisco carrying their bedrolls—and jelly jars full of gold. When the *Portland* arrived in Seattle a few days later, a newspaper greeted it with the headline "Ship with a Ton of Gold." The rush was on.

From a nation devastated by a depression, as many as a hundred thousand fortune seekers set off for the Klondike, not really knowing where it was or how to get there. Up to forty thousand stampeders crossed Chilkoot Pass or nearby White Pass to make their way down the Yukon River to Dawson City. Perhaps twenty thousand of them made it to Dawson, but few ever got a piece of the goldfield riches. Many soon returned home, rich only in a wealth of Klondike adventure.

in Santa Cruz, California, for $110. Then he spent the winter in Fresno, training his team to pull a homemade sled on wheels—a sight that must have struck the locals as odd.

Most of the gold seekers that spring of 1896 camped by the shores of Lake Bennett after completing the Chilkoot Trail. They built boats and waited for the ice to break up so they could float down the Yukon River to Forty Mile, or Circle City. But with Julian in the lead, the Berry party—including Ethel, and CJ's twenty-one-year-old brother Fred—got a jump on the other gold seekers. They mushed over the lake ice and down the frozen Yukon River, reaching the mining camp of Forty Mile months before the other prospectors.

Julian, fourth in line, helped Fred Berry to haul the lumber for the Berrys' cabins and sluice boxes on Bonanza Creek in 1898.

Cherubic children in the Far North pose with a mastiff, truly a gentle giant.

The English mastiffs of today are representatives of one of the oldest dog breeds, originating three thousand years ago in Egypt. The dukes of Devonshire and Sutherland developed English mastiffs in the eighteenth century, and these animals became popular among the nobility. They were used to hunt bears and wolves and to guard country estates. Since mastiffs were so large and expensive to keep, they became a sign of wealth. Among the middle classes, only the neighborhood butcher, who could feed a mastiff meat scraps, could afford to keep one. So mastiffs were often called "the butcher's dog."

Sometimes referred to as the canine "gentle giant," the mastiff can weigh 175 to 200 pounds on a frame up to thirty inches tall. Mastiffs have medium to short coats that are fawn, apricot, or brindle in color, with a black mask and ears.

In spite of its sometimes ferocious appearance, the mastiff has a docile temperament. At the same time, they are reliable watchdogs, taking unkindly to intruders. Renowned for intelligence, mastiffs require a lot of human contact, which Clarence and Ethel Berry certainly offered their mastiff Julian. They also need lots of space and plenty of exercise, which the Far North gave Julian in spades.

CJ took Julian up into the hills prospecting for gold, but they had no luck. Thus the Berrys were in Forty Mile in August when George Carmack arrived with news of his discoveries on the Klondike River near Dawson City. CJ and his brother Fred made the sixty-mile trip upriver to Dawson in only two days, bringing Julian and the rest of the team. Beating the crowd to the site, CJ staked Claim No. 40 on Bonanza Creek. He later traded it for shares in a rich claim on Eldorado Creek that turned out to be one of the richest in the Klondike. When the snow fell, the team led by Julian hauled cabin logs and lumber for sluice boxes.

And Julian became more famous still. He broke the record for pulling the heaviest loads of any dog in the Klondike. A massive animal, he was coveted by many other prospectors, and CJ was offered fabulous sums for the dog. But to him, Julian was a companion on the trail, a member of the family. CJ called him "old boy," and fussed over him, carefully changing the leather socks that protected his feet on the icy trails. He would not part with his faithful servant, and turned down all offers.

By the summer of 1897, the newlywed Berrys, who were $5,000 in debt when they left California, had $130,000 in gold dust and nuggets stored in a little shed. If anyone came near, Julian would warn the Berrys with barks and growls. One secret of their wealth was that CJ never stayed long enough in Dawson to get distracted at the saloons and gambling tables. Ethel was waiting back at the mine, and there was always work to do.

In 1897 the couple headed back to Fresno, California, for a much-needed rest, while Fred Berry and Julian remained in the Klondike to look after the claims. But Julian was soon suffering from rheumatism brought on by his labors at the mining camp. In 1898 the Berrys, who had returned to the Klondike, sent him to Fresno for medical treatment—and retirement. When the climate in Fresno became too hot for him, he was sent to the Pacific Coast, where—as the Fresno paper reported—"he will have an opportunity to try the Santa Cruz beach for his health."

The Berrys spared no expense for Julian's welfare, but he never completely regained his health. He died in May 1900. "Most Famous Dog in Alaska is Dead," said the headline for Julian's obituary in the *San Francisco Call*, as the Berry family mourned the loss of their beloved dog.

A massive animal, he [Julian] was coveted by many other prospectors, and CJ was offered fabulous sums for the dog. . . . CJ called him "old boy," and fussed over him, carefully changing the leather socks that protected his feet on the icy trails. He would not part with his faithful servant, and turned down all offers.

MOUNTIES AND THEIR DOGS

RCMP Kessler hikes through Yukon forest with one of his husky pack dogs, still important to the Mounties' work in 1938.

While they usually relied on horses, the Canadian lawmen known as the Mounties quickly realized the benefit of dogs for their work in the Far North. When news of the Klondike gold rush reached Ottawa, the Yukon field force of the North-West Mounted Police (later named the Royal Canadian Mounted Police) was dispatched to keep order.

Mounties were stationed at the summits of Chilkoot Pass and White Pass, at posts along the Yukon River, and at their headquarters in Dawson City. They also patrolled the trails, often using sled dogs in their work. By 1898, members of the Yukon field force had almost 150 dogs working for them. By the following year, the total was well over 200. The Mounties came to rely on local Natives as dog drivers and guides, especially on their long Northern patrols, and as special constables in remote areas.

The fictional hero Sergeant Preston with his famous dog companion, Yukon King, came to represent the myth of the Northern Frontiers.

Now as howling winds echo across the snow-covered reaches of the wild Northwest, the Quaker Oats Company, makers of Quaker Puffed Wheat and Quaker Puffed Rice, the delicious cereal shot from guns, presents Sergeant Preston of the Yukon. It's Yukon King, swiftest and strongest lead dog of the Northwest, breaking the trail for Sergeant Preston of the North-West Mounted Police in his relentless pursuit of lawbreakers.
—Introduction to the show
Sergeant Preston of the Yukon

Fictional Mounties have been popular since the pulp fiction days of the late 1890s, but none was more popular than Sergeant William Preston and his wonder dog, Yukon King. Stars of a long-running radio program and later a television show, Sergeant Preston and King always got their man. Sergeant Preston also had a horse named Rex, but Yukon King was the show's true hero. He saved the day by mauling crooks and hauling down villains. At the end of each week's

ordeal, Sergeant Preston was generous in his praise: "Well, King, thanks to you, this case is closed."

The story of Sergeant Preston began as a juvenile radio adventure series titled *Challenge of the Yukon,* which ran from 1938 to 1947 on a radio station in Detroit. The voices and situation were familiar to radio fans of *The Lone Ranger* and *Green Hornet,* for many of the same actors and writers worked on all three shows. When ABC radio picked it up in 1947, the show became a national hit. It was renamed *Sergeant Preston of the Yukon* in 1951 and ran until 1955, followed for three more years by the CBS television show of the same name. Old-time radio fans can still hear the words of Sergeant Preston as he urged his dogs onward, once each week, through the snowy wilderness: "On, King! On, you huskies!"

Like Sergeant Preston, the pulp fiction Mounties were always the good guys who captured the villains with the help of their faithful dogs. The bad guys often mistreated their own dogs, which contributed to their sorry end. In a 1931 story by Ryerson Johnson, called "The Dangerous Dan McGrew," a Mountie named Jim vowed to give an evildoer his comeuppance: "Jim's eyes gleamed. Sled dogs were man's best friend in the North; it made his blood boil to see the animals so cruelly treated. Well, he counseled himself grimly, after tonight these dogs would have an easier time."

Though these fictional stories about the Mounties were exaggerated, the portrayal of the Mounties' dependence on their dogs was accurate and a true testament to the value of a dog in the Northland.

GOETZMAN PHOT

Chapter 3

NERO

BIG DOG, BIG HEART

elinda Mulrooney, richest woman in the Klondike, was famous in Dawson City, and thus so was her dog. Their every move was followed, as noted in the *Klondike News* of April 1, 1898, at the height of the gold rush:

"Miss Mulrooney is a modest, refined and prepossessing young woman, a brilliant conversationalist, and a bright business woman. She makes the 18-mile trip to Dawson in a basket sleigh drawn by her faithful dog Nero, a noble animal of the St. Bernard breed and the largest dog in the Northwest. The trip is made in less than three hours."

In 1962 when Belinda was interviewed in a Seattle rest home on her ninetieth birthday, she dismissed as insignificant her part in the Klondike gold rush, her adventures in Dawson, and her years of living in Europe. But tears came to her eyes as she remembered her faithful friend in Dawson City, her big St. Bernard, Nero. Perhaps she was thinking back to her days of traveling the rough trail from Grand Forks to Dawson with Nero, as it wound through the valley of Bonanza Creek, passing the mining works of a hundred claims.

The miners who frequented her Grand Forks Hotel with its restaurant and bar paid in gold dust. Belinda was making so

◄◄◄ *The town of Grand Forks sprang up around Belinda Mulrooney's two-story log Grand Forks Hotel, at the far left in this photo taken in September 1899.*

◄◄ *Nero, a powerful purebred St. Bernard, was said to have been a model for Jack London's Buck in* The Call of the Wild.

▲ *Nero shows his affection for his owner, Belinda Mulrooney, in this rare photo from 1898.*

Nero was a rarity: a big St. Bernard in the Klondike. When Belinda Mulrooney constructed her hotel in 1898, she built a special kennel in the basement for Nero.

The St. Bernard is a large, intelligent dog descended from mastiff stock that was introduced into the Alps by the Romans two thousand years ago. Tall and massively boned, the St. Bernard is dignified in expression and carriage. The animal has a short, square muzzle, a muscular neck, and droopy eyes.

Developed during the seventeenth century by monks in the monastery of St. Bernard in the Swiss Alps, the dogs were trained to rescue travelers lost in the mountains. With its keen sense of smell, the St. Bernard could find people who were buried in the snow. The dogs were also trained to guide travelers over treacherous trails, giving warning of dangerous footing.

The St. Bernard is also valued as a watchdog. Some say this dog requires strong handling when on a leash. They do not mention that if the dog is like Nero, it can be a regular escape artist, pulling out chains or breaking ropes.

much money that her biggest problem was how to get it to the bank in Dawson. She would trust the trip to no one but herself and Nero.

On one trip in the spring of 1898, after the snows melted and with the creeks at their spring flood stage, she loaded Nero with two sacks of gold dust, one poke on each side. Belinda herself carried a poke on her back. As they approached one rushing stream, Belinda walked ahead and carefully crossed the wet log that served as a bridge. But when big, clumsy Nero got onto the slippery log, his legs flew out from under him. With a big splash, he landed in the creek.

Without the heavy pokes on his back, he might have been able to swim. But the weight of the gold began dragging him under. Belinda ran back to help.

Climbing up into a small willow tree, which bent under her weight, she leaned out over the water until she could just reach Nero's collar and keep his head out of the stream.

But there she was stuck! She couldn't move without letting go of Nero, and if she let go, Nero would surely drown.

Just then some miners came down the trail. "Cut the gold off the dog," Belinda yelled. "Just save the dog!" But the miners were more interested in saving Belinda than the dog. They tried to tie Belinda to the tree with a belt so she wouldn't fall off. But when one of the men climbed out onto the tree, it broke. With a crack and a splash, Belinda landed in the icy stream.

Floundering around with her big, wet dog, she managed to cut the gold pokes off Nero and he was able to scramble up the bank to safety. The gold was lost, but Nero was saved.

Nero had been "all ears, legs, and lanky body" when Belinda first saw him as a puppy in 1897. Then in her mid-twenties, she was already operating a restaurant in the new boomtown of Dawson. She had been raised in Pennsylvania, but as a very young woman made her way west and north, seeking business opportunity in the new mining towns.

The big, shaggy puppy belonged to an Englishman who had just arrived in town. The young man could not afford to feed the hungry pup, for he had lost everything when his boat swamped in the Yukon River.

She couldn't move without letting go of Nero, and if she let go, Nero would surely drown. . . . She managed to cut the gold pokes off Nero and he was able to scramble up the bank to safety. The gold was lost, but Nero was saved.

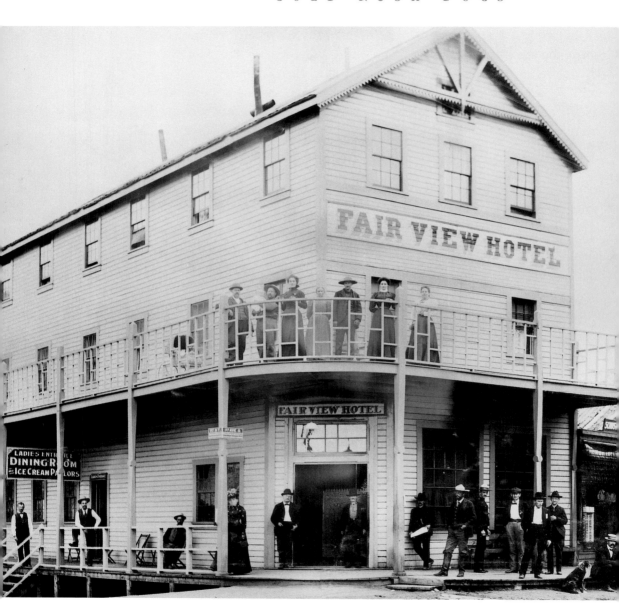

Belinda Mulrooney's elegant Fairview Hotel in Dawson City in July 1898.

So Belinda and the Englishman struck a deal. She would care for the pup and help the man find a job at a gold camp. At the end of the season, whomever the dog wanted to stay with would be the owner.

NERO

By the time the man returned from his season's work of shoveling gold into sluice boxes out on the creeks, the pup was devoted to Belinda. The dog became her closest companion. Under her care he filled out, and by the time winter came he was big and strong. One of the restaurant patrons dubbed the dog Nero, a reference to his large size and regal attitude, like the Roman emperor.

Belinda's first big success came with the hotel she built at Grand Forks. As the Klondike gold rush heated up, she also built a three-story hotel in Dawson City, called the Fairview. It was the fanciest hotel in town, and newcomers were astonished to see real china and linens on the tables, a chef from San Francisco, and crystal chandeliers. The basement was outfitted for her miner friends from the creeks, with lines above the big wood boiler for drying their clothes and a kennel for their dogs. The basement was Nero's home, too.

With her two hotels, Belinda was soon a rich woman. She decided to celebrate her success with a visit to her family in Pennsylvania.

Sadly leaving Nero in his usual spot in the basement of the Fairview Hotel, Belinda boarded the steamer headed up the Yukon River. A crowd of well-wishers stood on the riverbank to see her off on her trip Outside, as they referred to anyplace outside Alaska or the Yukon.

Suddenly there was Nero, dashing through the crowd and jumping into the river with a great splash. The people began to cheer him on: "Don't let her go, Nero!"

Nero swam for all he was worth, but the current took him downstream away from the boat. Miners aboard the boat urged the captain to help them get Nero, so he cut the engines and let the boat drift. The miners grabbed Nero and hauled him aboard through a low door on the engine deck.

"Any dog who wanted to go Outside so bad that he'd risk his life should have a trip," one of the miners said.

"Any dog who wanted to go Outside so bad that he'd risk his life should have a trip," one of the miners said. . . . And so Nero was on his way with his mistress.

Continued on page 47

The 1903 book cover, The Call of the Wild.

Jack London's fictional dogs Buck and White Fang have entertained and mesmerized millions of readers for the past century. The young writer from California spent only one season in the Yukon gold country, in 1897, but the immense popularity of his books based on this experience continue to influence the popular view of the Klondike.

In *The Call of the Wild,* published in 1903, the hero is Buck, a St. Bernard. The two dogs most often said to be the models for Buck were Nero, Belinda Mulrooney's St. Bernard, and Julian, Clarence Berry's mastiff. Both were huge dogs, capable of pulling great loads, as Buck did. And both were devoted to their owners, as Buck was to his kind master in the story, John Thornton. In the sequel *White Fang,* the animal is three-quarters wolf and one-quarter dog—with all the intelligence of a dog and the slyness of a wolf. London

portrayed the inner lives of Buck and White Fang in very human terms, and as separate from that of their owners.

While many dogs of the gold rush were loved and cared for, London chose to portray a dark conception of the life of these animals, using it to illustrate a human theme. London believed that the search for gold led men to revert to the most debased and animalistic sides of their characters—that within the primitive conditions of the Klondike, natural instincts for evil took over.

In *The Call of the Wild,* Buck is stolen from the congenial home of a doctor in California. Mistreated, his spirit broken, he is placed with a team of dogs hauling supplies into the gold rush town of Dawson City. Buck learns that in his new life, the rule is survival of the fittest, and he becomes willing to do anything to stay alive. Only when Buck joins up with Thornton, a trapper and woodcutter, does London portray a happy side to life. But in the end, Buck gives in to what London sees as his instincts and breaks away to the wilds to become leader of a pack of wolves.

In *White Fang,* London's taste for violence and his emphasis on primitive instinct again come to the fore. The wolf-dog White Fang endures a brutal owner, and the book relates scenes of beatings, hunger, and fighting. White Fang is eventually rescued by a kind man who takes the dog to California, where he becomes a hero saving his master's life.

As with *The Call of the Wild,* the story of *White Fang* has some basis in fact. Many dogs in the North had wolf blood, and many were certainly vicious. Some of the old-time mushers would beat their dogs, and in times of human famine, the dogs often went hungry as well. And dog fights were well chronicled in the Yukon. However, London's portrayals of the darker side of the rush for riches tell only part of the story, and also include troublesome and very limited stereotypes of both women and Native people.

In spite of ill health most of his life, London wrote nineteen novels and eighteen books of essays and short stories. He died in 1916, at the age of forty. *The Call of the Wild* and *White Fang,* translated into more than thirty languages, have sold millions of copies.

Who saved Smith's life May 20th 1899 on Otter Lake.

DOG WANTED

"Who saved Smith's Life" is the caption on this unusual photo of an unlikely sled dog.

With the great rush to the goldfields of Alaska and the Yukon, the competition to secure dogs to help haul loads was fierce, as a publication called *The Chicago Record's Book for Gold Seekers* explained:

In Seattle, Tacoma, and Portland, dogs . . . have become more valuable than horses. This unique condition of affairs results from the great and growing demand for dogs to be used in hauling sledges in the Yukon country and Alaska. . . . Good-sized dogs are bringing $15 to $30 each in the local markets. . . . At Juneau their value is double that sum, and on the Yukon River a good dog brings from $100 to $150. To the Yukon miner the dog has become what the reindeer is to the Laplander and the pony to the cowboys of Texas and Mexico.

45

From 1904 until his death in 1920, Hudson Stuck, the Episcopal archdeacon of the Yukon, traveled thousands of miles in his work as missionary to the Athabascan people of Interior Alaska and the Yukon Territory. From his base in Fairbanks, Stuck mushed dogs in the winter and traveled the rivers in the summer. His book *Ten Thousand Miles with a Dog Sled* chronicles the adventures of his winter tours.

Stuck's favorite dog was Nanook, who was tragically killed by the sharp kick of a horse's hoof in a stable at Circle Hot Springs. Reminiscing about Nanook, Stuck wrote:

> It was a pleasure to come back to Nanook after any long absence—a pleasure I was used to look forward to. There was no special fawning or demonstration of affection; he was not that kind; that I might have from any of the others; but from none but Nanook the bark of welcome with my particular inflection in it that no one else ever got. "Well, well; here's the boss again; glad to see you back"; that was about all it said. For he was a most independent dog and took to himself an air of partnership rather than subjection. Any man can make friends with any dog if he will, there is no question about that, but it takes a long time and mutual trust and mutual forbearance and mutual appreciation to make a partnership. Not every dog is fit to be a partner with a man; nor every man, I think fit to be a partner with a dog. Well, that long partnership was dissolved by the horse's hoof, and I was sore for its dissolution.

Hudson Stuck, Episcopal archdeacon of the Yukon, stands with one of his sled dogs— possibly his favorite, Nanook.

NERO

And so Nero was on his way with his mistress.

At Skagway, Belinda and Nero boarded the *City of Topeka*, a ship that Belinda had worked on before she went North to the Klondike gold rush. She knew the crew would let her keep Nero on board. The first thing they did in Seattle was visit the Turkish baths, where Nero was bathed, then combed and dried with an electric dryer. Then they paraded down the street to the Rainier Grand Hotel.

Belinda tied Nero in the basement of the hotel so he would stay out of trouble. But before she even reached her room, she heard banging and clanging. Nero came bounding up the stairs, dragging the gate he'd been tied to.

Deciding it wasn't practical to take Nero all the way back to Pennsylvania, Belinda arranged to board him in a stable. But months later when she returned to Seattle, Nero was gone. He had run away.

Belinda looked all over Seattle for Nero, even searching beneath the waterfront wharves. She stumbled between the wooden pilings, calling and calling for Nero. Suddenly there was a dirty and emaciated Nero looking up at her, crying and whining. After another Turkish bath and a few weeks of regular food, he looked as good as new.

Back in the Klondike, Belinda had caught the eye of Charles Eugene Carbonneau, a stylish champagne salesman from Quebec. Belinda reported that Nero liked Charles more than the dog liked anyone else in Dawson, besides herself. The couple married in 1900 and then set off for Paris, where they lived an elegant life for a few years while returning every summer to see to Belinda's business interests. Their marriage ended in failure after Charles began squandering much of Belinda's fortune.

The marriage and the move to Paris also meant a painful separation for Belinda and Nero. No one knows what happened to Nero after 1900. Belinda seemed to have put Nero out of her mind—until her ninetieth birthday, when the mention of her devoted old dog brought tears to her eyes.

Suddenly there was a dirty and emaciated Nero looking up at her, crying and whining. After another Turkish bath and a few weeks of regular food, he looked as good as new.

Chapter 4

YUKON

HIS MASTER'S GUARDIAN

Yukon stood guard in Skagway at the door of the Rev. R. M. Dickey's humble home, a crudely built lean-to attached to the Presbyterian Church. One after another, members of the town's vigilante committee arrived quietly. There were no police in Skagway, so the committee was meeting to plan how to rid the town of Soapy Smith and his gang of thieves and con men.

Yukon's owner was Skagway Bill Fonda, a veteran of gold rushes from California to Colorado to Canada. The group elected Skagway Bill the secret head of the new organization because of his experience with vigilante committees in the remote mining camps of California, high in the Sierra Nevada mountains. If Soapy's gang found out about their plans, they could infiltrate the organization, even kill Fonda. Skagway Bill depended on Yukon to alert him of danger as he went around town secretly recruiting people to join the committee.

Bill Fonda and his best dog, Yukon, were among the first to arrive in Skagway with the advent of the gold rush. Thousands of people landed at this Southeast Alaska town in the fall of 1897—ready to challenge Chilkoot Pass or White Pass, the routes to the Yukon River basin and its treasure. Like other experienced miners from all over the West, Bill wanted to be part of the next big strike.

◄ ◄ ◄ Men and dogs on the rough and rapidly thawing White Pass Trail in the spring of 1898.
◄ ◄ The treacherous mountain summit of the White Pass Trail.
▲ Yukon, a typical northern dog.

Nearly every prospector had a dog, for company as well as to help pull supplies.

No one knows exactly what kind of dog Yukon was. But he certainly fit the description of a one-man dog, as described by Hudson Stuck, who was the Episcopal archdeacon of the Yukon and leader of the first ascent of Mount McKinley in 1913:

> There is a dog, not uncommon in Alaska, that by a curious inversion of phrase is known as the "one-man dog." What is meant is the "one-dog-man dog," the dog that belongs to the man that uses only one dog. Many and many a prospector pulls his whole winter grub-stake a hundred miles or more into the hills with the aid of one dog. His progress is slow, in bad places or on upgrades he must relay, and all the time he is doing more work than the dog is, but he manages to get his stuff to his cabin or his camp with no other aid than one dog can give. It is usually a large heavy dog—speed never being asked of him, nor steady continuous winter work. . . . The companionship between such a man and such a dog is very close, and the understanding complete. Sometimes the dog will be his master's sole society for the whole winter.

Traveling with Bill was a young man named Frank Reid, whom Bill had befriended in Seattle. Reid was typical of the adventurous but naive men who hoped to make their fortune in the Far North. He didn't have the price of the boat fare to Skagway, so Bill hid him under his bunk and smuggled food to him on the trip up the Inside Passage.

ALL READY TO LEAVE SKAGWAY FOR A FAST
RUN THROUGH TO DAWSON. 600 MILES AWAY.

In Skagway, the two men and the dog—a forlorn-looking mutt—bunked in a cabin together, and Bill taught the young man the tricks of surviving in a gold rush town. Frank Reid was an experienced surveyor, so the men went to work making surveys of town lots and selling them. Bill and Frank also met the young minister who had been sent to follow the gold rush stampeders and help the unfortunate. While waiting for the passes to open, the Rev. Dickey decided that Skagway needed a church. So Skagway Bill went into the woods to cut trees for the project, and Yukon pulled them into town.

On a winter day in 1898, Yukon proved he had even more skills. It was during a time when high snows made the trail to

A diverse team of dogs sets off over the pass from Skagway with a passenger bundled in fur robes in the sled.

Yukon leading a team with Skagway Bill, left.

White Pass almost impossible to follow. Skagway Bill and a group of other volunteers headed out to mark the trail with tall flags. After they left Skagway, a huge blizzard blew in, and it snowed without letup for three days and three nights. Back in Skagway, Yukon waited for the return of his master. When the blizzard finally ended and the volunteers still had not returned, the Rev. Dickey and others set off to search for them, with Yukon in the lead.

"We must have been within a few miles of the summit when Yukon gave a strange whine and stood stock still—ears erect—listening," the Rev. Dickey later reported. "He began furiously scratching a hole in the snow pack, so we unpacked our shovels and began to dig a tunnel into the mountain of snow. After awhile we heard a faint answer to our calls. Pressing on we finally reached the entrapped men. Yukon's joy was unrestrained when he reached his master."

Continued on page 59

*The White Pass Trail came to be known as the Dead Horse Trail
because so many horses died over the winter of 1897–98.*

A sorry sidelight to the Klondike gold rush story was the frequent mistreatment of the horses used as pack animals over White Pass and on the lower approaches to Chilkoot Pass. Unscrupulous packers, eager to make a fast buck, often overburdened the animals and gave them little rest or food. The trails were treacherous, with jagged rocks and deep mud.

Traveler Peggy Shand was shocked by a confrontation with a desperate pack horse and its owner, who was forcing the exhausted animal to continue along the Chilkoot Trail at a point high above the Dyea River:

> With a supreme effort the frantic horse put forth its last ounce of strength. . . . The desperate creature could stand no more. She faced the cliff and deliberately jumped! Horrified I watched the horse fall through space and strike the water. . . . I felt like murdering the cruel man.

When journalist Emma Kelly came upon a group of starving, overworked pack horses on White Pass, she took direct action:

> They were simply racks of bones, scarcely any flesh upon their ribs. The five in the lead of the train gave out, and one which had fallen down was severely beaten by the cruel owner. The poor brute staggered to its feet, only to take a few steps, and then fell a second time. I watched the man as long as I could stand it, then ran over to my war-sack, got my revolver, and while he was at the rear of the pack-train, shot the animal in the head. I knew it was only a matter of a few hours before the poor beast would succumb, and I thought death would put it out of its misery.

After the White Pass & Yukon Route railway was built in 1899, many terrible hardships of the trail over that pass came to an end. But today passengers on the train can still look down into the gulch where the trail ran and see the whitened bones of horses that had died. The place became known as Dead Horse Trail.

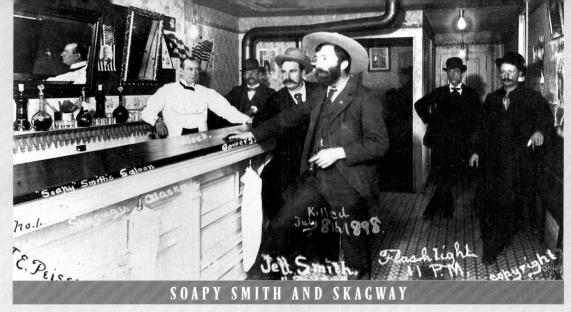

SOAPY SMITH AND SKAGWAY

The notorious criminal gang leader Soapy Smith poses at the bar of his famous saloon.

Skagway was indeed a wild town in 1897–98. Along with the gold rushers and prospectors came the worst elements of frontier society: the thieves, the crooked gamblers, the con men. Jefferson Randolph "Soapy" Smith organized such types into a gang that preyed on all of Skagway.

Soapy, who had already cheated the gullible from Butte, Montana, to Denver, Colorado, earned his nickname for the smooth way he practiced a famous con game. He would gather a crowd around him, pretending to sell a chance at winning a bar of soap wrapped in paper currency. His shills—people in the crowd who were secretly working with him—would put up some money and win a bar of soap wrapped in a fifty-dollar bill. Gamblers in the crowd would step up to try their luck, and of course they lost. He had raised his skill to an art by the time he arrived in the Colorado boomtown of Creede, a place so small that he and his cronies could control the entire town.

When Soapy and his gang heard about the Klondike gold rush, they envisioned more easy pickings. They settled on Skagway because of its fast growth, isolation, and lack of law enforcement. Some members of the gang practiced shell games and other fakeries, but the real secret of their success was working as an organized group. Some of them were steerers: men who looked trustworthy and directed newcomers

to fake businesses, including an infamous telegraph office where the gullible paid to send telegrams home, even though there was no telegraph line to Skagway. The group ran saloons, gambling houses, and brothels.

The citizens of Skagway soon decided something had to be done. Local businesspeople had a particular concern: the thieves were giving Skagway a bad name and were scaring off new travelers. The vigilante committee was formed, but Soapy's men infiltrated the meetings and intimidated anyone who dared to speak against them. When the gang grabbed one of the first returning stampeders, stealing all the gold he brought out of the Klondike, people of the town knew it was time to act.

Finally the night of July 7, 1898, the vigilante committee called a meeting at the end of the Skagway wharf. Frank Reid stationed himself as guard at the entrance to the wharf, and each committee member had to give the proper password. Soapy heard about the meeting and showed up. Reid challenged him, but instead of backing down, Soapy raised his gun. Both men fired. Reid was wounded, but Soapy was killed immediately.

Reid lingered nearly two weeks in the hospital before he died. Both men are buried at the Skagway Cemetery. "He gave his life for the honor of Skaguay," reads the marker on Reid's grave.

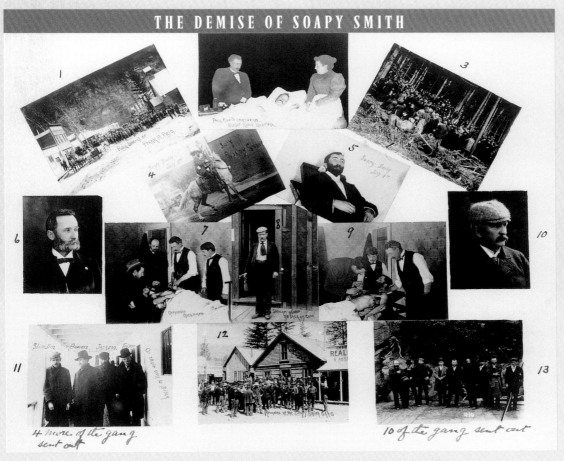

Collection of pictures depicting Soapy and his gang members.

At one point in his notorious life in Skagway, to improve his bad reputation, Soapy Smith established a fund to help the many dogs abandoned for the winter. But he couldn't forestall his inevitable end. Soapy's reign of terror and his subsequent demise became one of the most enduring tales of the gold rush. The story was enhanced by a pictorial series sold to tourists in Skagway through the years. Pictured are:

(1) Vigilante crowd gathered in the streets of Skagway;

(2) Frank Reid lingers in his sickbed;

(3) Crowd at Frank Reid's funeral at the Skagway Cemetery;

(4) Soapy on a white horse for the Fourth of July celebration in 1898;

(5, 7, and 9) Wake, and Soapy's autopsy;

(6) Unknown;

(8) J. D. Stewart, "the victim" whose fleecing was the final act that turned the populace against the gang;

(10) Frank Reid, Smith's killer and victim;

(11 and 13) Gang members banished from Skagway;

(12) Citizens gathered in front of City Hall to round up members of the gang.

Stampeders to the Klondike over the so-called "All-American Route" traveled straight up and over the Valdez Glacier that, at the time, extended nearly to tidewater directly in back of the old town of Valdez. The glacier has since receded almost four miles.

Two travelers, both named Joe Burke, were among the pioneers who negotiated the dangerous, futile route over the Valdez Glacier in search of a way to the Klondike goldfields. The first Joe Burke was a gold rush stampeder; the other was the dog he named after himself.

The glacier route from the coastal town of Valdez in Southcentral Alaska was being trumpeted by steamship companies as the "All American Route to the Klondike Gold Fields." All American it was, but the glacier led only to the Copper River Valley, a very long way from gold country. The few travelers who overcame the tremendous obstacles of glacier travel—snowstorms, avalanches, crevasses, frigid temperatures—and made it down the roiling Klutina River rapids to the Copper River found only disappointment.

After their trek across the glacier, the two Joe Burkes eventually settled in Valdez. With completion of the Richardson Highway and discovery of copper deposits, Valdez became a thriving port. When Joe Burke died, an obituary ran in the Valdez paper—confusing some people, not sure if the man were now dead. The obituary was for the dog.

Skagway Bill and the missing men had been buried under five feet of snow for three days. People gathered at the church to welcome back the successful search party and the missing, hungry men. All of Skagway hailed Yukon, the hero of the hour.

When the Rev. Dickey built his Skagway church, the workers added the lean-to on the back to serve as his home. And it was in this lean-to that the good citizens of Skagway finally organized to fight Soapy Smith and his gang. The secret committee tried to expose the gang, but no amount of effort seemed to be able to rid Skagway of the criminals, who became even bolder. Finally in a showdown on July 7, 1898, Bill's friend Frank Reid shot and killed the hated Soapy Smith. But by that time, Yukon and Skagway Bill, along with the Rev. Dickey, had moved on toward the Klondike.

At Lake Bennett, Skagway Bill got word that an old partner from California had staked a valuable claim in the Klondike. Bill took off with Yukon over the Yukon River ice in a dash to reach Dawson, where he staked a claim on Eureka Creek. But like many prospectors, Skagway Bill was happier looking for gold than actually mining it. When he didn't find gold after digging only fifteen feet down on his new claim, he gave up. He and Yukon traveled down the Yukon River to the military fort at Eagle, and then moved on to Circle City. Eventually man and dog made their way up to the Koyukuk River to join the gold rush there.

History loses track of Yukon at this point. Bill stayed in the Northland until 1919. Later he lived in Seattle, where he posed for the sculptor of the statue "The Prospector," which stands today in front of the Sitka Pioneers Home. Skagway Bill died at the home in 1938 at the age of eighty-two. Bill once wrote a poem titled "The End of the Trail," and perhaps it was partly in memory of the trusty dog who shared his many travels:

I must travel the miles till the journey is done,
Whatsoever the turn of the way;
I shall bring up at last at the set of the sun,
And shall rest at the close of the day.

Skagway Bill and the missing men had been buried under five feet of snow for three days. . . . All of Skagway hailed Yukon, the hero of the hour.

Lomen Bros.
Nome
#707

Chapter 5

FAUST

FEARLESS FRIEND

A small, dark-brown water spaniel with long, floppy ears was the unlikeliest dog to become a gold rush pioneer. Nevertheless Faust proved he was tough enough to survive on the hostile Seward Peninsula in Western Alaska. It does not appear that Faust made a pact with the devil, like his famous literary namesake, but both certainly experienced the wild life.

Faust and his mistress, Frances Ella "Fizzy" Fitz, arrived in Nome at the height of that region's gold rush in the summer of 1900. The nine-year-old spaniel had never seen such excitement. The beach was stacked high with goods and supplies and building materials, along with a sea of temporary tent dwellings. Businesses in tents and shacks lined the muddy streets, which swarmed with people looking to make their fortune. Music and shouting echoed at all hours from the saloons and dance halls. And unlike Dawson City, which was protected by the Mounties, Nome had no policemen at all.

Fizzy and Faust found a few empty square feet on the beach and set up their tent. Fizzy soon found a job as a typist, while Faust's job was to bark at intruders and to warn Fizzy when high tides threatened to flood the tent.

Faust accompanied Fizzy as she walked to her office every

◄◄◄ *Tents, lumber, and machinery lined the miles of beach at Nome, Alaska, circa 1900.*

◄◄ *Faust and Fizzy: The faithful Faust, a small American water spaniel, accompanied Frances Ella Fitz on a nearly fatal hundred-mile winter trek overland from Nome to the Fish River in 1900.*

▲ *Faust.*

Raggs was a cute stray puppy adopted by young, vivacious Nome hotel owner Edith Greta Crater, who later married novelist Rex Beach.

morning. Sometimes they had to step over drunks on the side-walks—or even the bodies of men who had been killed during the night. Working long hours, Fizzy soon had lots of money. But where could she hide it in this land of unsavory characters? She made a leather pouch for Faust to wear around his collar. Sometimes the dog roamed Nome carrying more than three thousand dollars in gold.

Fizzy had obtained Faust as a two-month-old puppy in Butte, Montana, in 1891. When the Butte economy plummeted with the closing of the copper mines, Fizzy went home to her mother and brother in New York City, bringing Faust with her. But when Fizzy heard about the gold strikes at Nome, she determined to head north. She bought a new outfit of warm clothes, and she and Faust took the train to Seattle to join the crowd boarding the ship *Tacoma* for Nome.

Fizzy was told that dogs had to travel in the hold of the ship. "But I wanted Faust with me," she later reported in her book, *Lady Sourdough*. "At the height of the jam, I concealed him as best I could, and hurried up the gangplank, and managed to sneak him into a storeroom on the hurricane deck."

Faust was an American water spaniel, a uniquely American breed developed in the upper Midwest. At the end of the nineteenth century the American water spaniel was one of the most favored hunting dogs in the country, especially in Wisconsin and Minnesota. With its dense, curly brown coat and muscular body, this dog was well-protected for working in cold Northern waters.

Effie is a modern purebred American water spaniel.

The American water spaniel of today is a medium-size, active dog between fifteen and eighteen inches tall at the shoulder, with a brown to chocolate-brown curly coat. Males weigh thirty to forty-five pounds, females twenty-five to forty pounds. It is a strong swimmer.

In 1986 the American water spaniel was designated the official state dog of Wisconsin.

The *Tacoma,* with Faust in his storeroom hideaway, made the rugged trip up through the Gulf of Alaska, then through the Aleutian Islands and into the Bering Sea. The ship, dodging icebergs, finally anchored a mile off Nome. Fizzy carried Faust in a pillowcase as she climbed down a rope ladder to a barge that took them ashore to their new life.

After a summer in Nome, Fizzy and Faust joined a group of men in December to explore gold claims on the Fox River, sixty miles from Nome. They expected the trip to Fox River to take seven days, but blizzards stretched the journey out to more than a month. Poor Faust! As the party waited out a blizzard in their tent, running low on food, the men began to talk of trapped miners who had resorted to eating their dogs. Fizzy made sure that didn't happen, figuring out ways for them all to survive on cornmeal and beans.

At the Fox River mining camp, they waited out the long, dark winter, looking forward to working on their claims in the spring. But with spring came a big surprise. As the ice on the river began its annual breakup, the river flooded their camp. Faust barked and

Miners lined miles of Nome beach, digging in the sand for gold.

growled as the water began flooding the cabin. At first Fizzy put Faust up on a bunk to keep him out of the water. As the flood waters rose, she and the dog found higher and higher perches inside the cabin. Finally they climbed out through a hole in the roof and managed to escape in a rowboat to high ground.

Faust and Fizzy later moved to the town of Council, where Fizzy got a job in the recorder's office. In big leather-bound books, she carefully wrote descriptions of mining claims that were filed. Faust could finally spend lazy days resting at Fizzy's feet or playing with the mining commissioner's two dogs.

One day as he wandered by himself only two blocks from the recorder's office, Faust encountered five malamutes pulling a sled. The malamutes chased him down the street at top speed, dumping their musher into the snow and smashing the sled. The dogs attacked Faust, but Fizzy and the commissioner were able to beat them back with a whip and a fireplace poker. Poor little Faust, wounded on his stomach, legs, and back, rested for days at home until he was well enough again to go out.

Rocking for Gold on Nome Beach, Alaska.

*Gold seekers on Nome beach used all manner of tools and equipment,
from simple gold pans to rockers, sluice boxes, conveyors, and novel inventions.*

The slow, traditional pace of life on the Seward Peninsula quickly became a thing of the past after three Scandinavian prospectors discovered gold in Anvil Creek near Cape Nome in 1898. When word of the strike reached Dawson, many stampeders who had failed to find gold in the Klondike floated down the Yukon River on their way to the new mining camp called Nome.

By the time they arrived, most of the claims were already staked by miners in the area. Stranded and destitute, hundreds of men, women, and children camped on the beaches. Then one morning in July 1899, the campers discovered that gold could be washed from the ruby-colored sands of the beaches. A "poor man's gold rush" ensued.

Nome was on the Bering Sea coast and, unlike the inland Klondike, could be reached by sea without the need to ever set foot on a trail. By the summer of 1900, twenty thousand stampeders had boarded boats in Seattle and headed for the new golden city. Many of them joined the crowds of people already camping on the beaches.

Exploration continued and gold was discovered in many creeks and valleys beyond Nome. Council City was established on the Niukluk River near the rich claims on Ophir Creek. Altogether, the creek claims, beach sands, and further discoveries yielded 4.8 million ounces of gold, and mining continues to this day.

Fizzy made some bad investments during her first two years in Alaska, but her luck changed when she staked a promising claim at

Hudson Stuck described the dog
Muk as a "pure malamute."

Of the malamutes, huskies, and Siberian huskies, the malamute is generally accepted to be the original Eskimo dog, named for an Inupiat tribe once know as the malamute.

"The best type of Yukon dog is the true Eskimo, known by the miners as "Malemut," from a tribe of Eskimo of that name at the mouth of the Yukon," wrote Tappan Adney, *Harper's Weekly* correspondent in the Yukon, 1897–98. "It stands about as high as the Scotch collie, which it resembles a little; but with its thick, short neck, sharp muzzle, oblique eyes, short, pointed ears, dense, coarse hair, which protects it from the severest cold, it is more wolf-like than any other variety of dog. With its bushy tail carried tightly curled over its back, with head and ears erect, and with its broad chest, it is the expression of energy, vitality, and self-reliance. . . .

"The best type of dog is still to be found among the Eskimos, as well as among the Indian tribes of the interior, but these latter . . . are frequently inferior in size, though they are very tough. . . . The 'inside' dog, as the native dog is called by the miners, endures hunger and cold better than the 'outside' [a non-Northern dog] and is therefore preferred for long journeys over the snow, where speed is desired and food is scarce or hard to carry or procure."

Describing a malamute, Adney says, "In harness he is really proud of his work, and trots along with . . . a happy contented 'smile.'"

As Tappen Adney described one malamute that belonged to famous dog driver Arthur Walden: "One of these dogs was a Malemut, jet black, with a bob-tail, and fur so thick that one can hardly separate the hairs to see to the skin. His fur is like that of a very thick black-bear-skin. He weighs eighty pounds, and he looks so much like a black bear that if a man saw him on the trail at a distance he would shoot him. He is as kind as a kitten, and loves to be petted, but is too heavy to get into Waldron's [sic] lap as he tries to do."

Ophir Creek. Faust spent the summer at the mine, playing among the pumps and the hydraulic nozzles. Thousands of gallons of water, shot through the nozzles, washed the gold-bearing gravel into the sluice boxes.

At cleanup time in August, when the equipment was shut down before winter freeze-up, Faust watched Fizzy and her men scrape

THE DOG'S HOME

Kennels, very much like barns, were built next to roadhouses for trail dogs, and in Nome for racing dogs.

Malamutes, huskies, and Siberian huskies all belong to the general classification of Northern working dogs.

Hudson's Bay voyageurs bred large domestic dogs like the Newfoundland and the St. Bernard with Native Indian dogs. The huskies that originated on the Mackenzie River in northern Canada were the forerunner of the common freight dogs of the gold rush. Weighing up to a hundred pounds, they are the largest of all husky breeds, developed as working dogs to pull heavy loads through deep snow.

The Siberian husky can be traced back to the region of Siberia, across the Bering Sea from Alaska. When residents of Nome developed dogsled racing in the early part of the twentieth century, they became more interested in a dog's speed and endurance than in its strength or pulling capacity. They traveled to Siberia to bring back smaller dogs with the desired characteristics. These dogs are the Siberian huskies.

Alaskans later went on to breed both working and racing dogs for strength, speed, and endurance. Sometimes they mixed hounds, pointers, setters, or collies with the Northern malamutes or huskies. New Englanders also became interested in racing, and dog fanciers there worked to standardize the Northern breeds and register them with the American Kennel Club.

A typical daily diet for the working dogs of the North would be fish, rice, and bacon fat. The food would often be cooked up into a stew and fed to the dog team.

Writer Tappan Adney reported on the menu during the early days of the Klondike gold rush:

A daily allowance for each dog while travelling was one cup of rice and one pound of bacon and one-half pound of fish at night. Dogs are fed only once a day. But sometimes when the men stop at noon to boil a kettle of tea and eat a doughnut, each is given a doughnut; but the rule is to give them all they can eat once a day.

Missionary Hudson Stuck reported that companies carrying the mail up and down the Yukon River by dogsled in the early 1900s spent about seventy-five dollars a year to feed each dog. Food costs were less for Native villagers with dog teams: They caught fish and fed some of it to the dogs.

Although dogs worked mainly during the winter, they had to be fed year-round. During the gold rush, a dog could be boarded for the summer at a Native fish camp for five dollars per month.

DOG PASSES AWAY

Fizzy and Faust mine for gold with a rocker on Fizzy's Ophir Creek claim, circa 1901.

Faust's obituary appeared in the *Seattle Daily Times,* May 3, 1906:

> Faust, one of the best-known dogs of the Seward Peninsula, died of old age at the residence of his mistress, Miss Frences E. Fitz, 1416 Minor Avenue, this week. Faust was 15 years old. He was a beautiful, brown-coated water spaniel of almost human intelligence. Born at Helena, Mont., he was one of twelve puppies. Since 2 months old he has been Miss Fitz' inseparable companion.

Few dogs of the United States or the Northland have had a more varied or picturesque career than Faust. As a show dog he traveled with the luxury of a prima donna over more than 25,000 miles in the United States before his advent to Alaska in the summer of 1900. He was the only dog ever permitted cabin passage on the steamship Victoria.

Despite a pampered life, he readily adapted himself to the rigors and privations of the Northland, travelling afoot through the snows of the winter of 1900 over the Great Divide to the mouth of Fox River. After encounters with Malamutes, the native dogs yielded to Faust's superior intelligence, and he became leader of a team, making many a record-breaking trip across country. He spent four winters in Alaska, coming out twice to Seattle.

A burial permit was granted Tuesday, and the last of "poor old Faust," as he was affectionately called in the Northland, was laid away in the dog cemetery beyond Beacon Hill.

*When the snow melted for the brief summer on Alaska's
Seward Peninsula, the miners used their sled dogs to pull innovative
"pupmobiles" on the railroad tracks out of Nome.*

All winter in Nome, local sled dogs hauled heavy, long freight sleds from town to the outlying mines, and then pulled the gold dust and nuggets back to Nome. In the summer, resourceful residents of the Seward Peninsula used their dogs to pull carts known as "pupmobiles" on the tracks of the Wild Goose Railroad. The original five-mile-long railway had been built in 1900 to haul freight from tidewater to Discovery Claim on Anvil Creek. The tracks extended nearly ninety miles by the time regular service was discontinued in 1910. Sometimes the dogs would be used to haul the pupmobile up hills, and then let free to run beside the tracks while the cart rolled down the hills. Baldy, Balto, and Togo all participated in this form of summer work, which also kept them in shape for winter hauling and racing.

the last of the gold from the bottom of the sluice boxes. Faust then trotted into the office with them, where they weighed out two thousand ounces of gold on the scales. All the hard work and difficulties had been worth it. Together, side by side, Fizzy and Faust had made their fortune.

The two companions were spending some time in Seattle when Faust died of natural causes in April 1906. Fizzy buried her loyal friend in the dog cemetery near Seattle's Beacon Hill. Faust, like the mastiff Julian before him, got his own newspaper obituary: Faust's death, and life, made the pages of the *Seattle Daily Times*.

SCOTTY AND BALDY

Chapter 6

BALDY

LOYAL LEADER

The cold wind blew fiercely, driving sharp, icy sleet into Baldy's face, but the dog pushed on. Musher Scotty Allan was depending on him. The storm worsened as Baldy and the rest of the team headed out of Spruce Creek. Blinding ice filled the air, and even Scotty couldn't find the trail.

With darkness approaching, Scotty got off the sled and moved Baldy and Kid into the front positions. Scotty had never chosen Baldy as a leader before. Then Scotty donned snowshoes and tromped out the trail in front of his team. The two lead dogs, harnessed in tandem, followed him up Topkok Hill. Straining with all his might, Baldy pulled the tug line connecting him to the rest of the team and the sled. Finally they descended the hill, through the clouds, with Baldy and Kid leading the team into Topkok, where a warm camp waited at the Timber Roadhouse.

Because of his daring move to push through this storm, Scotty Allan and his team went into the lead of the 408-mile All Alaska Sweepstakes in 1909. They eventually won the race from Nome to Candle and back in 82 hours, 2 minutes, and 41 seconds, giving Scotty his first victory and Baldy a new role as a lead dog. Even in the blinding snow, with ice caked in his paws, Baldy proved himself strong, faithful, and willing, qualities of a true leader.

◄◄◄ *Crowds gather on the streets of Nome to greet the victorious Bowen-Delzene team finishing the sixth All Alaska Sweepstakes race on April 10, 1913, in 75 hours and 42 minutes.*

◄◄ *Musher Scotty Allan cuts a dramatic figure in his elaborate Eskimo-made fur parka, as he poses with his famous lead dog, Baldy, around 1910.*

▲ *Baldy of Nome.*

Crowds line the streets for the start of a dog race in Nome.

Racing dogs in Nome were treated like thoroughbred race-horses in Kentucky. Their kennels were clean and modern and each dog had his own stall with fresh hay supplied daily. The dogs were well-known personalities, and often had human-sounding names. Among Baldy's kennel mates were the Tolman brothers, Tom, Dick, and Harry, legendary for their matched pace and endurance. Irish and Rover were purebred Irish setters, and Jack Macmillan had a reputation as the fiercest dog in Nome before Scotty tamed him.

Many of the dogs in the Darling-Allan racing kennels were mixed breeds of no particular distinction, and among these, Baldy

Baldy of Nome.

In the early part of the twentieth century, mushers used any kind of dog they could get. Many famous dogs like Baldy were mixed breeds. Even Baldy's biography—*Baldy of Nome,* by Esther Birdsall Darling—doesn't tell us what kind of dog he was. It simply reports that he was homely. But the book also says that Baldy was a pup from the Bowen-Dalzene Kennels, indicating that he really was bred for racing.

Throughout the past century, famous racing lines have relied on breeding with different types of dogs. Gareth Wright's famous Aurora huskies of the 1940s are said to have descended from a breeding accident with an Irish setter in Nenana. Musher Egil Ellis arrived in Alaska from Sweden in 1999 and began winning big sprint races with a team of huskies bred with German short-haired pointers. Mushers in Alaska prefer to breed their dogs for speed and endurance rather than simply to meet rigid kennel club standards for a particular breed.

was considered the homeliest. When co-owner Esther Birdsall Darling escorted visitors through the kennels, they invariably looked at Baldy and asked, "This isn't one of the racers, is it?" When she would say that he was, indeed, a racer, they would exclaim: "Well, he doesn't look it!" But Scotty always believed there was something special in Baldy, something that would come out with proper training.

Continued on page 81

ALL ALASKA SWEEPSTAKES 5TH ANNUAL

CANDLE AND RETURN · 360 MILES · ENTRANCE FEE $100.00

PURSE $5000.00 1ST $3000.00 2ND $1500.00 3RD $500.00 APR. 4TH 1912.

BOARD OF TRADE BULLETIN

The major dog race of the Nome season was the All Alaska Sweepstakes. Fans at the Board of Trade Saloon followed the progress of the racers as their times were called in by telephone and posted on the racing board.

Residents of Nome started the Nome Kennel Club in 1908 to improve the care and breeding of sled dogs. Albert Fink, formerly of Kentucky, was the first president. The club's racing rules became the model for all future sled-dog racing associations.

Following the lead of the great horseracing stables of Kentucky, the Kennel Club's events featured all the ceremony of the Kentucky Derby, including races started by heralds with bugles, and a race queen surrounded by her court. Each kennel had its own colors, featured on flags, pennants, and streamers, and even pom-poms for the dogs' harnesses. Crowds, including the children let out of school, cheered as their favorite team set off.

The club's premier race was the All Alaska Sweepstakes, the run from Nome to Candle and back each April—a distance that could be as long as 408 miles, depending on the route. Weather was always a factor: sudden blizzards, whiteouts, overflow on the rivers, and icy conditions were all potential hazards of the route. The Solomon Derby, on a 65-mile route from Nome to Solomon and back, was the second-most important event of the season. The shortest race, 6.3 miles from Nome to the Fort Davis Bridge, was a popular one for spectators on the beach. The annual high school race and the Ladies Race followed it. And in late spring, just before breakup of the ice in the rivers, came the Joy Race, in which each musher carried a passenger on a sled for 75 miles to the town of Council.

Gambling on the races was part of the scene. Telephone lines ran parallel to the courses, and reports from roadhouses, camps, and villages were phoned in and posted on the blackboard at the Board of Trade

WINNER SECOND PLACE.

RAMSAY'S ENTRY, 3RD ALL ALASKA SWEEPSTAKES, FOX RAMSAY, DRIVER.

COPYRIGHT, 1910
BY LOMEN BROS
NOME, ALASKA
#349.

Yours faithfully
C. Fox Maule Ramsey

Miner and sportsman Fox Maule Ramsey crossed the Bering Sea to Siberia and traveled up the Kolima River to obtain these Siberian huskies, which he raced in the 1910 All Alaska Sweepstakes, placing second.

Saloon in Nome. The sporting crowd spent race days gathered around the telephone and the racing board, waiting for the latest updates.

The science of dog mushing advanced greatly during those early racing years. Kennels developed the most effective ways to hitch up the dogs and the best materials to use in building sleds. They determined what qualities to look for in a lead dog and the best diets for the animals.

The Nome Kennel Club pioneered the open race format in which the number of dogs used to pull a sled is optional, leaving the decision to each musher. The club ruled, however, that no dog could be abandoned and that cruelty was prohibited. Drivers usually ran behind their sled, jumping on and off the runners, ready to push or balance the sled as necessary. Mushers' decisions on when to run and when to rest were an important element of strategy, just as they are today.

The first All Alaska Sweepstakes in 1908 was something of an experiment, as the first long-distance sled-dog race anywhere. A team run by musher John Hegness won the event. Scotty Allan's team of mixed-

breed dogs won the second race, but a team of Siberian huskies run by a trader named Goosak attracted attention during that event. Soon after, musher Fox Maule Ramsay traveled to Siberia and brought back a number of Siberian huskies, smaller dogs with legendary endurance.

A team of Siberian huskies won the race in 1910. But in 1911, Scotty Allan charged back to the victory stand, running a typical team of mixed-breed dogs. Scotty's last win came in 1912, though he placed third the following year and second in 1914 and 1915. Then came the Seppala years: Leonhard Seppala and his famous Siberian huskies won the final three runnings of the All Alaska Sweepstakes, in 1915, 1916, and 1917.

◀◀ *Cover, All Alaska Sweepstakes Souvenir booklet, 1909.*
◀ *All Alaska Sweepstakes trophy cup.*

*Scotty Allan with Baldy and his team of mixed-breed dogs was the
winner of the fifth All Alaska Sweepstakes race in 1912.*

Allan Alexander Allan, with his Scottish brogue, was
known through the North Country simply as Scotty.
As a boy in Scotland, he learned to train horses and dogs.
One year he won the Grand National Sheep Dog Trial.

In 1887 he traveled to the United States to deliver
a valuable Clydesdale stallion, and then as a footloose
young man held many jobs around the American West.
When he headed for the Klondike in 1897, he
temporarily left a wife and a two-month-old baby.
Thanks to his experience working with dogs, he was
able to establish himself in Dawson as a premier dog-
driver. His leader Dubby was a huge Mackenzie River
husky from the stock of the Hudson's Bay Company.
When Scotty followed the stampede to the next gold
strike, in Nome, Dubby led the way on a twelve-
hundred-mile run down the frozen Yukon River.

Scotty didn't strike it rich on his claims at Nome,
so he got a job as a clerk at the Darling and Dean
Hardware Company and sent for his family. In the first
All Alaska Sweepstakes, in 1908, Scotty drove a team
from the J. Berger Kennels. The next year he won the
race, again driving a Berger team—now including
Baldy. By the fourth race, Scotty was driving for his
own kennel, which he ran in partnership with Esther
Birdsall Darling.

"Dogs are the most intuitive creatures alive,"
Scotty once said. "They take the disposition and
feelings of their driver. That is why I never let my dogs
know I'm tired. At the end of the day when my heart
has been nigh breaking with the weariness, I sing to the
little chaps, and whistle, so they always reach the end
of the trail with their tails up and waving."

Scotty's skills as a trainer were put to their most
important use during World War I when a young
French lieutenant, Rene Haas, saw a need for trained
dogs in the war effort. Haas, who knew of sled dogs
because of an earlier visit to Nome, asked Scotty to
secretly purchase one hundred dogs for the French
army. Scotty secured the dogs—along with sleds,
harnesses, and two tons of dried salmon—and brought
them to a training site in Canada, where they joined
three hundred Canadian dogs. Scotty then trained
French army personnel in working with the animals in
teams that could pull loaded sleds. In the Vosges
Mountains of France, the dogs soon proved their
worth. They carried ammunition to a French military
unit in an isolated valley, hauled telephone wire for
stringing behind German lines, and helped in the
evacuation of wounded soldiers.

After the war and a term in the territorial
legislature, Scotty and his family, including Baldy,
moved to California. Scotty and Fay Dalzene, another
Nome Sweepstakes winner, promoted dog mushing in
California at a number of winter resorts. He later
acquired dogs in Nome and trained them for Admiral
Richard Byrd's 1928 Antarctica expedition. After Byrd's
trip, Scotty sold the animals to breeders in New
England as the perfect sled dogs, and they became the
breeding stock for registered Alaska malamutes.

Scotty died in 1941.

BALDY

So from puppyhood, Baldy was included in the fall training regime. The dogs were taken on runs of increasing length, until one hundred miles seemed like a comfortable afternoon jaunt. Training continued until the height of the season, the All Alaska Sweepstakes in April. Baldy's performance soon proved that Scotty was right about him.

Baldy's most famous moment came during Nome's Solomon Derby sled-dog race. Scotty hitched Baldy up in the lead, and at the crack of the starting pistol, they took off. The dogs were flying along the trail, only a few miles before the turnaround point at Solomon, when Baldy missed the soothing sound of Scotty's voice. Baldy stopped the team and discovered that Scotty was no longer with the sled. Snarling slightly at the other dogs to make sure they knew he meant business, Baldy wheeled the team around and led them back a short distance down the trail.

"Baldy of Nome."
"Scotty" Allen's famous Leader,
Winner of $25,000⁰⁰ in Sweepstake prizes.
© Winter & Pond Co.
Juneau, Alaska.

There along the trail lay the still form of Scotty, blood from a head wound staining the snow. While leaning down to adjust the sled's brake, he had been struck by an iron trail marker and knocked off. Baldy licked his master's face and kept whimpering and barking until Scotty woke up and dragged himself into the basket of the sled.

"Turn around, Baldy, and head for Solomon," Scotty whispered, urging the dog to continue the race. Amazingly they were the first team to arrive in Solomon, where Scotty's friends took one look at the gash on his forehead and urged him to quit. But he wouldn't listen. "Baldy and I can make it," he said, and off they went. Sailing into Nome, Scotty and Baldy claimed the derby prize.

▲▲ *Scotty Allan.*
▲ *Baldy; Baldy's paw print. Esther Darling personalized a copy of her novel* Baldy of Nome *with Baldy's paw print.*

While the Inupiat Eskimos of the Seward Peninsula had always relied on work dogs, they were not generally active in the dog races staged by the white community in Nome. But when the gold rush and an interest in sled-dog racing moved to the Interior, the Athabascan Indians of the Yukon and Tanana Rivers came to prominence in the sport. The Athabascans had always used dogs to help them in trapping, hunting, and hauling firewood. And when holidays came to the villages, the celebrations sometimes included dog races.

Athabascan drivers from the villages—like Joe Stickman of Nulato and Johnny Allen—were among those who competed in the annual sixty-five-mile Signal Race from Fairbanks to Livengood and back. Stickman was a winner throughout the 1920s and Allen won three times in the 1930s. Then, in the 1950s, Horace Smoke captured the imagination of the public by becoming the first to win the race three times in a row—and with the same lead dog each time.

These hearty racers from the Interior mushed their teams upriver from the villages to Fairbanks, a

Athabascan Horace Smoke was the celebrated winner of the North American Sled Dog Race in Fairbanks in 1951.

four- or five-day trip. "They didn't have big kennels then," recalls Effie Kokrine, one of the first women to win the Signal Race. "They just used their village dogs, their work dogs. They borrowed dogs from other people in the village, too."

Effie and her husband, Andy, were in the first wave of village mushers to move to Fairbanks, taking advantage of job and educational opportunities. The Kokrine family followed Gareth Wright of Nenana, who started his kennels in Fairbanks in 1947, beginning what would become one of Alaska's most famous dog lines. Also among the big names of racing in that era was a whole roster of Athabascan mushers: Bergman Kokrine, Harold Woods, Marvin Kokrine, Charlie Titus, Walter Riley, Bergman Sam, Warner Vent, Cue Bifelt.

In the 1960s, competition got much stronger as racers like Roland Lombard came up from the Lower 48 states with fast dogs, and they were tough to beat. George Attla, the famous "Huslia Hustler," was one of the first Athabascan mushers to catch the new spirit and start racing faster. He notched multiple wins in sprint races like the North American Championship Sled Dog Race in Fairbanks and the Fur Rendezvous Race in Anchorage.

By the late 1960s, as snow machines replaced village dog teams, Native involvement in sled-dog racing was on the wane. But with creation of the long-distance Iditarod Trail Sled Dog Race®, Native mushers got back into the thick of it. Inupiat musher Isaac Okleasik, from Teller, won the sprint race in 1967, precursor to the first full Iditarod race several years later. Okleasik won with his team of large working dogs.

Carl Huntington, an Athabascan from Galena, won the second running of the Iditarod, in 1974. Athabascans Emmitt Peters, from Ruby, and Gerald Riley, of Nenana, were the Iditarod winners in 1975 and 1976, respectively. Inupiat Herbie Nayokpuk, the "Shishmaref Cannonball," was a formidable competitor who finished the Iditarod numerous times.

As the popularity of big races increased, so did the cost of competing. Mushers today compete in an era when top drivers maintain kennels of fifty or more dogs and costs continue to spiral upward making sled dog racing a specialized sport.

THE WOMAN

Author and poet Esther Birdsall Darling lived in Nome from 1907 until 1917.

Esther Birdsall Darling was an avid dog fan and co-owner with Scotty Allan of the famous Darling-Allan racing kennels. She came to Nome in 1907 as the wife of Ned Darling, an owner of the Darling and Dean hardware store. In her first book, *Baldy of Nome,* published in 1913, she not only immortalized Baldy but also captured the spirit of the people of Nome and their reverence for their dogs. Reflecting the writing style of that period, the book gives Baldy human-like thoughts and feelings.

Baldy was already known for his racing prowess, but with the success of the book, he became more famous still. Darling then wrote books about Baldy's descendants, including *Navarre of the North* and *Boris, Grandson of Baldy.* The books were popular with both adults and children, and by the 1950s, *Baldy of Nome* was in its seventeenth printing.

Darling also produced two adult novels, *The Luck of the Trail* and *The Break-up.* Her poetry was widely published in the North, and her poem about the forget-me-not influenced the Alaska legislature to select it as the state flower. Esther Birdsall Darling died in California in 1965.

Scotty Allan and Baldy won the All Alaska Sweepstakes in 1909, 1911, and 1912, placed second in 1914 and 1915, and finished third in 1913. When Scotty was elected to the Alaska Legislature after World War I, he and Baldy mushed twelve hundred miles from Nome, then boarded a boat in Cordova to travel to Juneau for the legislative session. Baldy was so famous by this time—he was even the subject of a popular book, *Baldy of Nome*—that when he arrived in Juneau, tourists tried to cut off a piece of his fur for a souvenir.

Baldy's dogsled days were now over. Scotty got Baldy a mate named Laska, and after one legislative session in Juneau, Scotty and his family—including Baldy and Laska—moved to California. During a happy retirement, the two dogs became parents of many puppies.

⇥ THE WINNERS. ⇤
FINISH LEONHARD SEPPALA ENTRY, 9TH ALL AL
NOME ALASKA ADDY WITH

LomenBros.
Nome.
#629B

EPSTAKES,
E6, 80 Hours, 38 Mi..5 Sec.

"TOGO"

Chapter 7

TOGO

BORN TO LEAD

Togo was perhaps the most famous Alaskan Siberian husky that ever lived. His owner, Leonhard Seppala, said that in Togo he finally found the natural-born leader he had tried for years to breed. Togo had great speed and endurance, and he had such a masterful sense of direction that he could always find his way in a storm.

He also had the ability to trace a straight course—a skill that was a mixed blessing. On a circular course, he would invariably try to lead the team in a beeline across the track—in his mind, the shortest and fastest way to their destination. On a trail down a twisting and turning river, he would often make a dash up the bank and try to lead the team through the willow trees in search of a shortcut.

Togo was born in 1913 at the Seppala kennels in Little Creek, outside Nome. He was a spoiled pup, hard to handle, difficult, and mischievous. Seppala sold Togo when he was first born, but the owner returned the dog because he was too much trouble. Seppala then found a second owner—but Togo jumped through the window of his new mistress's cabin and ran back to Little Creek. Seppala gave in and accepted the dog as part of his kennel.

He let the young Togo run alongside as he trained his dog team that fall. In November, Seppala had to make the long trip to Dime

◀◀◀ *Leonhard Seppala and his team of Siberian huskies won the ninth All Alaska Sweepstakes— 408 miles in 80 hours, 38 minutes, and 5 seconds—on April 14, 1916.*

◀◀ *Togo, a Siberian husky, was Leonhard Seppala's lead dog in many winning racing teams and for the serum run to Nome in 1925.*

▲ *Togo, one of the heroes of the Nome serum run.*

Togo, a Siberian husky.

Togo was a Siberian husky, a direct descendant of the Siberian dogs brought to Alaska in 1910 by musher Fox Maule Ramsay. Smaller and faster than the more common malamutes, Togo and his teammates won race after race in Nome and elsewhere.

The dogs brought from Siberia had been bred there by the indigenous Chukchi people to pull light loads at moderate speeds and to survive on relatively little food. Commonly run in large numbers, teams comprised sixteen to eighteen dogs.

The Siberian huskies of today are powerful, medium-size working dogs with striking almond-shaped blue eyes and a heavy fur coat. They range in height from twenty-one to twenty-three inches and weigh forty-five to sixty pounds. This breed was officially recognized by the American Kennel Club in the 1930s, and the first registered Siberian was a direct descendant of Togo. Registered Siberian huskies are popular as show dogs in the eastern United States, but the racing huskies of Alaska represent a mixture that is bred for speed and endurance rather than for kennel-club purity.

Creek. He tied Togo up in the dog corral, since at eight months of age he was too young to be harnessed into the team. But Togo had other ideas. After the team left, he jumped the seven-foot fence around the corral and disappeared into the darkness of a winter blizzard.

The next morning, Togo stood waiting as Seppala left the road-house where he and the team had stayed overnight. There was no way to send him back, so Seppala got out an extra harness and let Togo run with the older dogs. Still a puppy, he traveled seventy-five

The Eskimo-made fur parka and mukluks were part of the famous dog musher mystique cultivated by Norwegian Leonhard Seppala, who became well-known for his dog driving exploits on the Seward Peninsula.

miles. After that trip, Togo showed he could work harder than any of the other dogs. Before long he was promoted from wheel dog (the beginner's position directly in front of the sled) to leader. He stayed at the front of Seppala's team for the next sixteen years.

Seppala trained his team hard for the 1915 All Alaska Sweepstakes race, getting the dogs in top shape by hauling freight and passengers around the Seward Peninsula all winter. People considered his team,

*In a few short years,
Togo and Seppala
won the All Alaska
Sweepstakes three
times, the Ruby
Derby twice, and a
variety of other races.*

with Togo in the lead, a long shot because Seppala's Siberian dogs were much smaller than the big malamute freight dogs and the other racing dogs. But Seppala and his team won the event, arriving more than an hour in front of veteran Scotty Allan.

Togo and Seppala later set off with the team for the Yukon River town of Ruby, where they won the Ruby Derby. In a few short years, Togo and Seppala won the All Alaska Sweepstakes three times, the Ruby Derby twice, and a variety of other races.

Togo's speed and leadership helped in a brave attempt to save a life in the winter of 1916–17. Seppala and his team had just pulled in to Dime Creek with a passenger named Stevenson when townspeople told him fellow musher Bobby Brown had been mangled at his sawmill there, with one leg nearly cut off. They knew Seppala and his dogs stood the best chance of getting Bobby to the hospital in Candle in time to save his life.

They put Bobby in the sled, with Stevenson also on board to help the injured man. Seppala and his dogs took off in the intense cold and blowing snow, with Bobby wrapped in wolf robes, leaning against Stevenson. It was late in the afternoon, and the team had had little rest that day. The village of Candle lay sixty-two miles to the north. If the sled turned over on the rough trail, Bobby could bleed to death. In spite of the darkness and a growing blizzard, Togo set a fast pace and kept the team on the trail.

Finally at eleven o'clock, Seppala spotted the lights of the hospital, and Bobby was quickly turned over to a doctor's care. In spite of the safe, speedy trip and the doctor's best efforts, Bobby died a few days later. But this courageous "run against death" still made a great impression on the people of Nome and of all Alaska.

Togo made an even more remarkable run in January 1925, when a diphtheria epidemic hit Nome and the serum needed was a thousand miles away in Anchorage. Conditions were so severe, with temperatures at fifty degrees below zero, that the airplanes of the day couldn't make the trip. So the people of Nome turned to their most famous and reliable musher and his lead dog to obtain the serum. Seppala and his team headed east for the Athabascan village

In January 1925, Nome was still as isolated as it had been during the gold rush days a quarter-century earlier. Supplies for the town's three hundred residents were delivered by ships that arrived only during the short summer season when the pack ice left the shore. In winter, mail still arrived by dogsled. So when Dr. Curtis Welch discovered a case of deadly diphtheria among the isolated inhabitants, he knew an epidemic—and a panic—could ensue.

During the late 1800s, epidemics of this contagious bacterial disease swept across the United States and western Europe, killing thousands of people, mostly children under the age of ten. Widespread immunization began in 1920, and the disease almost vanished. Yet even though diphtheria had become rare, it was no less fatal.

Dr. Welch had come to northwestern Alaska in 1906, and in all that time had never seen a case of diphtheria. He had none of the antitoxin serum that would fight the disease, and the closest supply was clear across the Territory of Alaska, in Anchorage. For winter travel in that era, only dog teams could be counted on to make the journey, and thus began the great serum run of 1925.

The serum was first sent some three hundred miles by train from Anchorage to Nenana. Wild Bill Shannon, waiting with his sled and dog team, took possession of the precious serum, which was packed in a twenty-pound cylinder wrapped in insulation. Nome lay 674 miles to the northwest. Shannon and his dogs left Nenana on January 27 at 11 P.M. and drove 52 miles through the night to Tolovana, where musher Edgar Kalland waited.

Kalland mushed 30 miles, then passed the serum to Dan Green at Manley Hot Springs. Green took it to Fish Lake, 28 miles away, where Johnny Folger waited. Then Sam Joseph mushed seven malamutes to Tanana, at the junction of the Tanana and Yukon Rivers. At each stop along the way, the package of serum was warmed, just as doctors had instructed.

From Tanana, a series of drivers—Titus Nikolai, Dave Corning, Harry Pitka, Bill McCarty, Edgar Nollner, George Nollner—took their turns relaying the serum down the frozen Yukon River from village to roadhouse, roadhouse to fish camp.

At Nulato, Tommy Patsy picked up the serum and delivered it downriver to Kaltag, where the trail left the broad highway of the Yukon River and headed over a mountain pass to the village of Unalakleet on Norton Sound. An Athabascan river pilot known only as Jackscrew started off from Kaltag with a dog team, and later passed the serum to Victor Anagick, who reached Unalakleet at 3:30 A.M. on January 31.

From here, Myles Gonangnan drove his team due north up the shore. At Shaktoolik, Henry Ivanoff took over. Fifteen miles out, Ivanoff met Leonhard Seppala and his dog team led by Togo, who then headed toward Nome with the serum. At Golovin, Charlie Olson and his team took over, fighting their way through fifty-mile-an-hour winds and temperatures of minus thirty degrees to Bluff, where Gunnar Kaasen began the final leg to Nome.

The serum run captured the imagination of the world, and newspapers followed the progress of the faraway mushers via telegraphed reports. Kaasen and his lead dog Balto arrived in Nome with the serum on February 2. Dr. Welch began inoculations immediately. Instead of a massive outbreak, he was able to contain the disease and limit the deaths to those of three children. By February 21 the diphtheria threat had ended.

While the serum run drew the world's attention to the importance of dog mushing in the Far North, in an ironic twist it signaled an end to the sled-dog era. After the serum run, the U.S. Post Office worked to institute air mail delivery. When the mail was delivered by dog team, the drivers supported a network of roadhouses and fish camps that kept the trails open. But with air delivery, the trails fell into disuse. More and more people began traveling by airplane and, later, snow machine, and dog teams were no longer a necessity.

The dramatic effort of dogs and mushers during the serum run remains a memorable part of Alaska history, commemorated each year in the Iditarod Trail Sled Dog Race® that follows much of the same route.

As a young man, Leonhard Seppala traveled from his native Norway to Nome, urged there by his countryman Jafet Lindberg, one of the discoverers of the Anvil Creek claims that started the Nome gold rush. In the summers, Seppala worked at Lindberg's mines. In the winters, he traveled on skis or with a dog team to check out new strikes on the Seward Peninsula. Seppala didn't discover gold, but he made a name for himself as a dog driver, ferrying people and supplies to far-flung mining camps.

Seppala's career as a dog musher took off when Jafet Lindberg gave him a team of fifteen small but sturdy Siberian huskies to train. This unusual team of smaller dogs attracted attention, and he was urged to compete in Nome's All Alaska Sweepstakes race in 1914. He ended up dropping

out when the first experimental run with his young team didn't pan out. But the next year, Seppala surprised everyone when he beat the favorite, Scotty Allan, for the trophy. It was only the first of many victories for Seppala and his lead dog, Togo.

Between racing seasons, they piled up long miles transporting people over much of bush Alaska. Seppala and his team took a businessman from Nome to Fairbanks, and they transported a young woman adventurer from Fairbanks to Nome. They traveled from Nome to Iditarod, McGrath, and Anchorage with Major Gotwals of the Alaska Road Commission, investigating road and trail projects in the fall of 1916.

Seppala and his team went on to win the All Alaska Sweepstakes again in 1916 and 1917. But

of Nulato on the Yukon River, where they were to meet a musher carrying the serum up from Anchorage.

After Seppala set out, the plan changed in hopes of a speedier

World War I and the declining fortunes of Nome combined to reduce the town's population. Only three teams entered the sweepstakes in 1917. After that, Seppala worked in Nome for a large gold-dredging company, once again ferrying people and supplies. Then came the great serum run of 1925, including the magnificent effort put forth by Seppala and Togo. For a brief few weeks, the world's attention focused on Nome and the racing dogs of Alaska.

Afterward everyone wanted to see the famous dogs. Seppala took Togo and his team on an extended U.S. tour. Eventually Seppala settled Togo into retirement in Maine and he returned to Alaska, where he became superintendent of the Davidson Ditch, a sixty-five-mile-long waterway

Leonhard Seppala, left, and his winning team after the tenth and last All Alaska Sweepstakes in 1917.

that carried water for mining operations near Fairbanks.

In the winters Seppala traveled to New England, where dog fans staged an active racing season. His efforts culminated in a first-place finish in the Eastern International race in Quebec and participation in the dog races featured as a demonstration sport at the 1932 Olympics in Lake Placid, New York. After his retirement in 1946, Seppala and his wife, Constance, moved to Seattle, where he died at the age of ninety in 1967.

serum delivery. The Northern Commercial Company organized a relay from the end of the railroad in Nenana, near Fairbanks, so that each musher heading toward Nome would have to cover only a

An epic poem by Esther Birdsall Darling commemorates the attempt of Leonhard Seppala and his dog team led by the Siberian husky Togo to save the life of Bobby Brown. After Brown was severely injured in an accident at Dime Creek in the winter of 1916–17, Seppala and a man named Stevenson rushed him through darkness and storm to the hospital in Candle. An excerpt:

> For at Dime there was crushed in a moment,
> Bobby Brown, well beloved far and wide;
> Whose life ebbing fast strikes the driver aghast,
> As he faces his harrowing ride.
>
> There's the broken and pain-tortured body
> Lying heavy on Stevenson's lap;
> There are unuttered fears and his friends' bitter tears,
> As they fasten each buckle and strap.
>
> Then the swift-spoken word to the leader,
> While as swiftly he answers the same:
> "There's a race to be run, and a stake to be won—
> Come, Togo, live up to your name!"
>
> There's the sting and the rage of the blizzard,
> as the arctic unleashes its gale;
> there's the night falling gray at the end of the day,
> And there's Death riding hard on their Trail.
>
> Man's pluck, and the strength of a dog team—
> "On Togo! We trust to your pace."
> There's the flash of a light—then there's Candle in sight—
> And Seppala beats death in the Race!

relatively short distance before the serum was taken over by a fresh team and driver.

Wild Bill Shannon, the first driver, left Nenana on the night of January 27, heading west with a team of malamutes. After a series of relays using fifteen drivers and teams, the serum was transferred at the Norton Sound village of Shaktoolik to Henry Ivanoff.

Just fifteen miles out of Shaktoolik, Ivanoff surprised Seppala, who was coming from Nome. Seppala still thought that he was to pick up the serum at Nulato and return to Nome. Instead, Ivanoff handed the serum to Seppala, who turned his dogs around and headed north, back toward Nome.

Togo's uncanny sense of direction now made the difference as he led his team on a shortcut over the ice of Norton Bay. In spite of a wind-whipped ground storm, the team covered the forty-two miles to Isaac's Point at an average speed of more than seven miles per hour. There Seppala waited for the weather to improve. Instead it grew worse.

Not wanting to delay any further, Seppala headed Togo and the team into the gale and drove on to Golovin. They had now covered the longest and most difficult part of the serum run. When they turned the serum over to Charlie Olson, Nome lay only about eighty miles away over familiar trails. In their run from Nome to their meeting with Ivanoff and then back again toward Nome, Seppala and Togo had traveled a total of 260 miles.

But Togo did not emerge as the canine hero of the serum run. That honor went to Balto, the leader of the last team, the one that actually delivered the serum to Nome. But glory or no glory, the miles had taken their toll. Togo was now twelve years old, and the serum run was his last in Alaska.

Seppala took Togo and the team on a tour around the United States, even appearing on the ice during halftime at a series of hockey games in New York's Madison Square Garden. They entered sled-dog races in New Hampshire and Maine, winning time and again and becoming a popular attraction.

Finally, after a lifetime of running more than five thousand miles, Togo was ready for a New England retirement. Seppala left him with Elizabeth Ricker at the Ricker-Seppala Kennel in Poland Springs, Maine, where she developed a line of purebred Siberian huskies descended from the famous dog. Togo died there in 1929 at the age of sixteen. The body of this Alaska hero was later preserved and is now on view at the headquarters of the Iditarod Trail Sled Dog Race® near Anchorage.

Seppala headed Togo and the team into the gale and drove on to Golovin. They had now covered the longest and most difficult part of the serum run. When they turned the serum over to Charlie Olson, Nome lay only about eighty miles away over familiar trails.

Chapter 8

BALTO

HERO OF THE HOUR

No one who knew him could ever imagine that Balto would one day be honored with a statue in New York's Central Park. Schoolchildren by the thousands now play on the statue and learn through books and movies of Balto's famous run to bring diphtheria serum to Nome. But Balto was just an ordinary freight dog—a "work horse," you might call him.

Balto lived in one of Leonhard Seppala's kennels and worked for a Nome mining company. No one would have thought to run him in a dog race—certainly not his owner, Seppala, who ran a string of matched Siberian racing dogs. Balto was probably not even a typical sled dog. He was thought to be a Norwegian or Lapp reindeer dog, or *Lapphund,* that Seppala bought from a reindeer herder.

With his fellow working dogs, Balto labored during the winters pulling a sled full of freight for the mines and the big gold dredges out on the creeks. In summer he pulled the "pupmobile," a wheeled wagon that ran on the tracks of the Nome Railway. Balto simply did his job hauling loads until the serum run in 1925.

In January of that year, Seppala harnessed up Togo, his favorite lead dog, and organized the rest of his racing team to help rush diphtheria serum to the endangered town of Nome. When the call went out for more drivers to put together dog teams to help relay

◄◄◄ Balto leading Gunnar Kaasen's team on First Avenue in Nome, 1925.
◄◄ Gunnar Kaasen poses in his fur garb with Balto on a publicity tour after completing the final leg of the serum run to Nome.
▲ Balto.

The Lapphund came to Nome and the Seward Peninsula with reindeer herders from Scandinavia. Missionaries had arranged to import reindeer herds from Siberia as a food source for the Inupiat Eskimos, after the supply of whales and other sea mammals was severely depleted by whaling fleets. The herders were members of the Saami, or Lapp, people.

The Lapphund developed in the Arctic and circumpolar regions. With a heavy coat, small ears to reduce the risk of frostbite, and a bushy tail that acts like a blanket in the snow, the dogs are well-adapted to the North. The Norwegians, Swedes, and Finns, who shared with the Saami the northernmost reaches of the Scandinavian Peninsula, also adopted the dogs and today there are many varieties.

the serum on the 674-mile route from Nenana to Nome, Gunnar Kaasen responded.

Kaasen worked for Seppala as a dog driver. And while Seppala didn't think Balto was fast enough for the job, Kaasen sensed unusual qualities in the dog. He noticed Balto's endurance, loyalty, and intelligence, and he knew he would do whatever was asked of him. For lead dog on his team, Kaasen chose Balto.

From Nome, Kaasen drove his team fifty-three miles east to the roadhouse in Bluff to wait for the serum. Balto growled when he heard musher Charlie Olson pull in, carrying the serum that he had received from Seppala at the relay point farther east, at Golovin. The temperature was twenty-eight below zero, with a raging wind. But Kaasen, a hardy Norwegian, hitched the dogs to the sled, packed the serum inside a caribou hide, and took off into the storm.

Balto led the team through blinding snow to Solomon. If they had stopped to rest, Kaasen would have gotten the message to wait out the storm. But Balto and Kaasen passed by Solomon without even realizing it. At 2:00 A.M. they reached Point Safety, ready to turn the serum over to the next musher, Ed Rohn. However, Rohn was asleep, believing that Kaasen had stopped at Solomon to wait out the storm. So Kaasen mushed on with his tired team, covering the final twenty-two-mile stretch through whiteout conditions into Nome.

When they arrived at 5:30 A.M. on February 2, even Dr. Curtis Welch, the physician who was desperately waiting for the serum,

Percy DeWolfe, one of the most famous mail drivers in the Yukon, was known for the care that he gave to his dogs.

was asleep. No one expected the relay to be completed in only 127 ½ hours. Newspapers and newsreel movies throughout the world were drawn to the story, and as leader of the dog team that delivered the serum to Dr. Welch, Balto was lauded as the hero of the "great race of mercy."

Kaasen and Balto and the rest of the team were invited down to the Lower 48 states, where they were cheered in parades. Money was raised for the statue of Balto in Central Park. But as the weeks went on, the country's attention shifted to other things. Kaasen got an offer to cast Balto and the other dogs in the movies, but after just one film, the producers no longer wanted the dogs. Months later they ended up as a sideshow attraction in a Los Angeles "dime museum."

When George Kimball, a traveling salesman from Cleveland, saw the dogs at the museum, he was shocked to discover that they weren't even well fed. Determined to rescue them, he enlisted the help of the people of Cleveland. With backing from the *Plain Dealer* newspaper and pennies from Cleveland schoolchildren,

The mail carriers who made their deliveries by dog team quickly became Northern heroes. In summer, mail and freight arrived by boat or packhorse. But in winter, dogsleds carried the load.

Early carriers were paid one dollar per letter, plus an extra commission on any gold they transported. Teams of eight to ten dogs pulled loads weighing eight hundred to a thousand pounds, and the mail teams always had the right of way.

A system of roadhouses, really just crude cabins, were built at an average of every fifteen miles along the trails. Each night when the mail carrier reached a roadhouse, he unhitched his dogs and fed them before doing anything else. Then he brought the lead dog inside to sleep under a bunk, while the other dogs curled up outside on beds of hay, covering their noses with their bushy tails before settling in for a night's sleep.

In 1899, Big Ben Downing, not having much success finding gold in Dawson City, established the first mail route down the Yukon River. His dogs traveled the rough ice of the Yukon through the winter snows from Dawson to eventually deliver mail to the new gold camp of Nome. He kept more than a hundred dogs in a corral near Dawson, and was always ready to trade or buy a good dog. During an interview, with a husky's forepaws on his shoulder as the dog tried to lick his face, Downing said: "I always did love my dogs."

Canadian Percy DeWolfe, who delivered the mail

from Dawson City to Eagle for thirty-five years, was known as the "Iron Man of the North." Each fall, before the winter delivery season, DeWolfe supplied his cabins and way stations with thirty tons of hay, dog food, and groceries. His 102-mile mail route took eight days—four days each way. An international dog-team race between Dawson and Eagle was inaugurated in 1977 to honor DeWolfe.

Mail carrier Ed Biederman made the winter run between Eagle and Circle for over thirty years. He and his huskies mushed forty-two hundred miles each winter to fulfill their mail contract, which called for thirteen round trips. In 1938, Biederman lost the mail contract to the airlines, and the day

Prior to the airplane, Alaskans depended on dog teams to deliver the mail in the winter. Here, a larger than average mail team leaves the Copper River town of Chitina.

of the dogsled mail carrier soon came to an end.

The site of the old Biederman fish camp at Charley River now serves as a checkpoint for the Yukon Quest sled-dog race. The Biederman family donated one of his dogsleds to the Smithsonian Institution. It's now part of a Postal Service exhibit in Washington, D.C., that commemorates the part played by hardy huskies of the North in carrying the U.S. mail.

Balto and Kaasen pose with the statue of Balto erected in New York City's Central Park in 1925. Balto died in Cleveland in 1933.

Kimball raised enough money to bring the dog team to his city.

In March 1927, Balto and his teammates marched through downtown Cleveland in a welcoming parade. Soon they were comfortably settled in quarters at the Cleveland Zoo. When Balto died six years later, his body was preserved and put on display in the Cleveland Museum, where it remains today. The affection that children still hold for Balto reflects the love that so many people feel for brave animals that accomplish so much more than we might expect of them.

Iditarod racers head for the finish in Nome.

Trumpeted as "The Last Great Race," the Iditarod Trail Sled Dog Race® is run annually in March from Anchorage to Nome along a course that covers more than eleven hundred miles. The race commemorates the 1925 dogsled run that delivered diphtheria serum to Nome, and it covers much of the original route.

The Iditarod Trail Sled Dog Race® got its start from an idea by Dorothy Page, chairwoman of the Wasilla-Knik centennial committee. She wanted to have a race as part of the centennial celebration of the purchase of Alaska from Russia. Page found her most enthusiastic supporter and promoter of the race in Joe Redington Sr., a musher from the Knik area.

The 1967 event was a big success, even though it covered only twenty-eight miles. In 1973, amid plenty of comments that it couldn't be done, Redington and Page organized the first Iditarod Trail Sled Dog Race® to Nome.

In that first running, twenty-two mushers and their dog teams finished the course, with the winner taking nearly three weeks. Today the winners cover the same course in only ten days. Weather remains the major obstacle. Temperatures can drop to sixty degrees below zero, but they can also rise enough on a warm spring day to make snow on the trail too soft to travel.

From Anchorage, the trail crosses the Alaska Range and heads through untamed backcountry to the Yukon River. (The old gold rush town of Iditarod, namesake for the race, is on the route in odd-numbered years; the race takes a more northerly course in even-numbered years.) The route then travels the Yukon River before crossing the mountains to the coastal village of Unalakleet. The race finishes with a long dash up the coast to Nome, with mushers and their teams often facing sixty-mile-an-hour winds and snow squalls, or dense fog.

Schoolchildren, dog lovers, and race fans from around the world follow the Iditarod, checking on their favorite mushers and dogs via Internet and radio reports from checkpoints along the trail. The Iditarod is the best known of the annual long-distance sled-dog races of today, which also include the thousand-mile Yukon Quest between Fairbanks, Alaska, and Whitehorse, Yukon Territory, and the Kuskokwim 300 out of Bethel, Alaska.

Chapter 9

PATSY ANN
PRINCESS OF THE PIERS

Patsy Ann waited at the Pacific Steamship dock for the ship to arrive. She stood on guard, her white, compact body not moving a muscle, her thick neck pointing out, her small eyes squinting at the horizon. This would be the first boatload of supplies for Juneau and its big gold mines in more than two weeks. Somehow Patsy Ann always seemed to know when and where each ship would dock. Townspeople were waiting at the other landing facility, the Alaska Steamship Dock, but Patsy Ann waited it out alone—until the ship sounded its whistle and pulled in at her dock. Patsy Ann was right again.

Patsy Ann, a bull terrier, showed up in Juneau sometime in the late 1920s, at a time when the huge Alaska Juneau Mill was still extracting gold from ore found beneath Mount Roberts. Did Patsy Ann jump ship when a boat she was on delivered supplies to Juneau? Or did she arrive with a new doctor or businessman in town, but run away because she could not get along with his children? Whatever the true story, Patsy Ann lived on her own in the bustling port town. People in her adopted town treated her well: maybe they felt sorry for her when they discovered she was deaf.

Patsy Ann became a beloved figure on the docks and streets of Juneau, and stories about her were told and retold in barrooms and

◄◄◄ Juneau street scene, circa 1920.
◄◄ Docks in front of A.J. Mine. Juneau, with its valuable gold mines, was accessible only by ship.
▲ The gold rush was long over by 1930, but the sentiment of Alaskans for dogs lived on in the warm affection Juneauites and tourists felt for Patsy Ann, an independent-minded bull terrier.

*Children in the mining town of Douglas, across the channel
from Juneau, use their dogs to pull sleds in 1912.*

Gold has its place in the rich history of the Juneau area in the form of several large commercial mining operations. The Treadwell mine on Douglas Island near Juneau became one of the most valuable gold mining operations in the world in the 1890s. Gold-bearing ore was at first mined from one huge pit called the Glory Hole, and then from tunnels beneath the sea.

To extract the gold, more than five hundred of the half-ton iron implements known as "stamps" pounded the ore almost a hundred times per minute—creating a roar like thunder, twenty-four hours a day. Three other mining operations later opened, and together the four mines employed nearly three hundred men.

Some of the miners, who were simply working for wages, got gold rush fever when they heard about free placer claims farther north. Some of them headed over the Chilkoot Pass or White Pass in order to prospect in the Yukon basin, site of the Klondike strike in 1896.

The Treadwell operation prospered until 1917, but by then it was nearly mined out. Following several cave-ins, the ground in front of the mine buildings suddenly dropped into a huge sinkhole. In a matter of minutes, buildings and machinery were swallowed up and seawater rushed in to fill the mine tunnels.

A new operation, the Alaska Juneau, opened in 1917 near Juneau to mine ore and extract its gold.

In the 1930s, while the rest of the United States slid into economic depression, Juneau reveled in a new prosperity brought on by an increase in the price of gold from less than twenty-one dollars to thirty-five dollars per ounce. By the late 1930s, the mine and mill employed more than a thousand men, working round the clock.

in newspapers until truth and fiction became intertwined. Tourists vied to take her photograph, cab drivers pointed her out as she trotted down the street, and Juneau's curio shops sold postcards with her picture.

In her early days in Alaska, Patsy Ann was often seen traveling independently. She frequently hopped aboard the little ferry that carried passengers from Juneau to the gold mines on Douglas Island. In a booklet about Patsy Ann, Laura McCarley tells a story of one summer when the dog got onto a ship that traveled north to Skagway, then walked onto a train of the White Pass and Yukon Route railway and ended up in Whitehorse. From there, she boarded the SS *Casca,* headed down the Yukon River to Dawson City. When the boat stopped to refuel at Fort Selkirk, Patsy Ann jumped off to chase rabbits and, as the story tells it, the passengers had to wait for three hours because the captain would not proceed until she was back on board.

Patsy Ann's favorite activity was to greet every ship that docked at Juneau. No matter how far she was from the docks, she always seemed to arrive in time to watch the ship come in. She greeted the sailors as they came ashore, and she barked a friendly greeting to the cooks, who found tasty morsels in the kitchen for her. When ships departed, she would sometimes jump into the water and swim after them for a bit.

Patsy Ann loved crowds and frequently attended Juneau's popular baseball games. Skagway ballplayer Louis Selmer told of one especially exciting game between Skagway and Juneau, when the score was tied and the bases loaded. Patsy Ann ran out on the field and wrestled the ball away from the Skagway pitcher. The game resumed only after Patsy Ann was finished with her play.

When the city of Juneau ruled that all dogs must be licensed, contributions poured in from Pasty Ann's fans—enough to buy her a license, along with a fancy collar to hang the new tag on. The city held a ceremony in 1934 to present Patsy Ann with her collar and license and to bestow on her the title "Official Greeter of Juneau."

Patsy Ann's favorite activity was to greet every ship that docked at Juneau. No matter how far she was from the docks, she always seemed to arrive in time to watch the ship come in. She greeted the sailors as they came ashore, and she barked a friendly greeting to the cooks, who found tasty morsels in the kitchen for her.

"*Princess Sophia*" ten hours after striking Vanderbilt Reef

A photo of the ill-fated Princess Sophia, *stuck on Vanderbilt Reef.*

Some say the tragic sinking of the *Princess Sophia* off Juneau in the winter of 1918 signaled an end to the gold rush era. The ship carried many residents of gold country, who had traveled aboard the last paddlewheeler up the Yukon River to Whitehorse before winter freeze-up and then journeyed on the White Pass railway to Skagway. Glad to have escaped the North before the icy lock-up of winter, the crowd boarded the *Princess Sophia*.

When the ship grounded on a rock in the channel near Berners Bay, the captain and passengers were alarmed but not desperate. But then a storm came up. The wind changed, and the ship suddenly slipped off the rock and sank. More than 350 men, women, and children lost their lives.

An Irish setter named Jack swam eight miles through the frigid water to shore. Half-starved and covered with oil, he was found by Auke Bay residents two days after the sinking. He was the only survivor.

Patsy Ann frequently slept at the longshoremen's hall on Willoughby Avenue. When the docks were quiet, she made the rounds of her favorite Juneau establishments. At the fire hall she visited the old-timers who hung out there. She often stopped by for meals at the City Cafe. In the summer she preferred the cool darkness of the Imperial Saloon, and in the winter she liked to curl up by the potbellied stove at the office of the *Empire* newspaper.

"PATSY ANN"
She never missed a boat.

T. Davis - Juneau

Patsy Ann was a favorite of the tourists who arrived in cruise ships, and all the shops sold postcard pictures with her title, "Official Greeter of Juneau."

In the 1800s, English breeders crossed the bulldog with the Old English terrier to produce the bull terrier. They soon became fashionable pets, favored by the gentry. These muscular dogs, with their short, flat hair and egg-shaped head, usually weigh about seventy-five pounds. Spirited and independent, they do not get along well with other dogs and prefer to run around on their own.

Like Patsy Ann, they do seem to enjoy human companionship. Alert and curious, bull terriers are more inclined to dig than other breeds.

Over the years they have been used as guard dogs, rat catchers, and herders. Although they are active and sturdily built, they should not be confused with the far more aggressive pit bull terrier.

At the beginning of World War II, Patsy Ann met her last ship. Then she returned to the union hall, where she curled up in a corner and died in her sleep, on March 30, 1942. She was given a loving funeral and buried in a hardwood box under the Alaska Steamship dock. Today a statue of Patsy Ann stands on the wharf, where she forever remains the official greeter, a reminder of Juneau's colorful gold rush past.

NOTES

Five dogs standing, Coffee Creek, 1930s.

See Information Sources for complete references.

PAGE 3 Epigraph from *Old Yukon,* by James Wickersham (Washington, D.C.: Washington Law Book Co., 1938).

INTRODUCTION Epigraph from *The Klondike Stampede,* by Tappan Adney (New York: Harper and Brothers, 1900).

CHAPTER 1 STICKEEN Ideas on Stickeen and the theme and general introduction of this book developed from reading Ronald H. Limbaugh's book and Malcolm Margolin's afterword to John Muir's *Stickeen.* Also helpful was Rennick.

CHAPTER 2 JULIAN William Berry graciously shared family stories, photographs, and archival materials on Julian. Information on the Mounties came from Helen Dobrowalsky.

CHAPTER 3 NERO Melanie Mayer provided prepublication manuscript pages with stories about Nero. The "Dog Wanted" quote is from *The Chicago Record's Book for Gold Seekers* (Chicago: Monroe Book Co., 1897).

CHAPTER 4 YUKON Yukon's story is taken from the writings of the Rev. R. M.

Dickey, rescued from obscurity, published, and shared with us by Art Peterson (*Gold Fever: A Narrative of the Great Klondike Gold Rush, 1897–1899,* by Robert McCahon Dickey. Auke Bay: Klondike Research, 1997). Dead Horse Trail: Margaret C. Shand and Ora M. Shand's *The Summit and Beyond* (Caldwell, Idaho: Caxton, 1959); Emma Kelly, "Women's Endurance in Alaska," *Outdoor World and Recreation,* Aug./ Sept. 1912. Thanks to Joe Leahy and the Valdez Museum for the story of Joe Burke. Information on Skagway Bill and poem, thanks to Stan Patty, Seattle.

CHAPTER 5 FAUST The story of Faust comes from *Lady Sourdough,* by Frances Ella Fitz (New York: Macmillan, 1941).

CHAPTER 6 BALDY The Nome Visitors and Convention Bureau staff, especially Lana Harris, were very helpful in developing the stories about the dogs of Nome and about Esther Darling, as was Laura Samuelson of the Carrie M. McLain Memorial Museum in Nome. Important books were *Baldy of Nome,* by Esther Birdsall Darling (New York: Alfred A. Knopf, 1951); *Navarre of the North,* a thrilling story of the grandson of Baldy, also by Esther Birdsall Darling (Garden

City, New York: Doubleday and Co., 1930); and Scotty Allan's autobiography *Gold, Men, and Dogs* (New York: G. P. Putnam and Sons, 1931).

CHAPTER 7 TOGO Important help came from the Nome Visitors and Convention Bureau and the Carrie M. McLain Memorial Museum in Nome. Books included *The Complete Siberian Husky,* by Lorna B. Demidoff and Michael Jennings, and *Seppala: Alaska Dog Driver,* by Elsie Rickers (Boston: Little Brown, 1930). For the serum run: William H. Wilson, "The Serum Dash to Nome, 1925." *The Alaska Journal,* 16: 1986. Darling's poem is in *Seppala.*

CHAPTER 8 BALTO A useful book was Natalie Standiford's. The Viking answer lady on about.com provided information on Norwegian Lapphunds.

CHAPTER 9 PATSY ANN The staff of the Alaska Historical Library in Juneau helped with the story of Patsy Ann, providing copies of booklets by Laura McCarley and Carl Burrows. The stories of the mail carriers owe much to Elva Scott in her book *Jewel on the Yukon: Eagle City* (Eagle City: Eagle Historical Society and Museums, 1997).

Mushing a bear.

FURTHER READING

Clifford, Howard. *The Skagway Story.* Portland: Alaska Northwest Books, 1988.

Demidoff, Lorna B., and Michael Jennings. *The Complete Siberian Husky.* New York: Howell Book House, 1978.

Dobrowalsky, Helen. *Law of the Yukon.* Whitehorse: Lost Moose Press, 1995.

Hutchison, Don, ed. *Scarlet Riders: Pulp Fiction Tales of the Mounties.* Oakville, Ontario: Mosaic Press, 1998.

Limbaugh, Ronald H. *Stickeen and the Lessons of Nature.* Fairbanks: University of Alaska Press, 1996.

Mayer, Melanie, and Robert N. DeArmond. *Staking Her Claim.* Athens, Ohio: Swallow Press, 2000.

Muir, John. *Stickeen.* Afterword by Malcolm Margolin. Berkeley: Heyday Books, 1981.

Murphy, Claire Rudolf, and Jane G. Haigh. *Gold Rush Women.* Portland: Alaska Northwest Books, 1997.

———. *Children of the Gold Rush.* Portland: Alaska Northwest Books, 2001.

Rennick, Penny, ed. *Dogs of the North.* Anchorage: Alaska Geographic, Vol. 14, No. 1, 1987.

Satterfield, Archie. *Chilkoot Pass: The Most Famous Trail in the North.* Portland: Alaska Northwest Books, 1980.

Sherwonit, Bill (text), and Jeff Schultz (photos). *Iditarod: The Great Race to Nome.* Portland: Alaska Northwest Books, 1991.

Standiford, Natalie. *Bravest Dog Ever: The True Story of Balto.* New York: Random House, 1989.

Stuck, Hudson. *Ten Thousand Miles with a Dog Sled.* New York: Scribners, 1914; and Lincoln: University of Nebraska Press, 1977.

Wood, Beverly, and Chris Wood. *Dog Star.* Victoria, B.C.: Polestar Book Publishers, 1997.

INTERNET RESOURCES

Alaska Native Studies Curriculum and Teacher Development: www.alaskool.org

Arctic culture: http://arcticculture.about.com/culture/arcticculture

American Kennel Club: www.akc.org/index.html

American Water Spaniels: www.starsouth.com/awsc

Author Jane Haigh: www.janehaigh.com

Author Claire Rudolf Murphy: www.clairerudolfmurphy.com

Balto site: www.dogsled.com/html/balto.shtml

Iditarod Trail Sled Dog Race®: www.iditarod.com/index.shtml

Mushing Magazine: www.mushing.com

Nome Convention and Visitors Bureau, Iditarod site:

www.alaska.net/~nome/iditarod.htm

Nome Kennel Club: www.nomekennelclub.com/links.htm

Norwegian Lapphunds, Viking answer lady: www.about.com

Patsy Ann site: www.patsyann.com

Royal Canadian Mounted Police: www.rcmpmuseum.com

Stickeen site: http://yosemite.ca.us/john_muir_exhibit/writings/stickeen

Threads of Gold exhibit, University of Alaska Museum: www.uaf.edu/museum/exhibits/tog/index.html

Yukon Historical and Museums Association: www.yukonalaska.com/yhma/index.htm

Joyce and Austin Menzies with Whitey.

INDEX

Dog team with airplane.

I N D E X

A C K N O W L E D G M E N T S

We would like to thank William F. Berry; Laura Samuelson at the Carrie McLain Museum in Nome; Lana Harris and the Nome Visitors and Convention Bureau staff; Kay Shelton and the staff of the Alaska State Library, Juneau; Sibylle Zemitis at the California State Library; Charlotte Jewell, Joe Leahy, and Pete Bowers; Bruce Merrill of the Alaska Room at the Loussac Library in Anchorage; Michael Burwell; Dave Neufelds; Jo Antonson; Dianne Brenner and Mina Jacobs at the Anchorage Museum of History and Art; the staff of the archives at the Rasmuson Library at the University of Alaska Fairbanks; and the research staff of the Noel Wien Library in Fairbanks. For photographs, Candy Waugaman was, as usual, unfailingly supportive and generous.

CLAIRE RUDOLF MURPHY has written more than fifteen books for children, fiction and nonfiction, including *I am Sacajawea, I Am York: Our Journey West with Lewis and Clark; Children of Alcatraz* and her latest book *Marching with Aunt Susan: Susan B. Anthony and the Fight for Women's Suffrage*. Claire has a passion for history, especially the untold stories of outsiders. During her years in Alaska, she taught language arts and drama, and worked with the Alaska State Writing Project. Currently Claire serves on the faculty of Hamline University's MFAC, a graduate creative writing program for children's writers. She lives in Spokane, Washington, where she enjoys music and outdoor activities with her husband. Her two grown children live in Seattle.

www.clairerudolfmurphy.com
www.thestorytellersinkpot.blogspot.com

Claire Rudolf Murphy, left, and Jane G. Haigh.

Alaska author and historian **JANE HAIGH** began her career as a local historian in Fairbanks where she completed an MA in Northern Studies at the University of Alaska Fairbanks. She was honored in 2007 as the Alaska Historian of the Year by the Alaska Historical Society for her most recent books, *Searching for Fannie Quigley: A Wilderness Life in the Shadow of Mt. McKinley* (Ohio University Press, 2007) and *King Con: the Story of Soapy Smith* (Friday 501 Books, 2006). Jane recently completed a PhD in U.S. History and American Indian Studies at the University of Arizona in Tucson and has joined the faculty at Kenai Peninsula College, in Soldotna, Alaska.

www.janehaigh.com

GOLD RUSH WOMEN

ISBN 978-0-9627530-5-3, $16.95

"Alaska: where the men are men and the women are left out
of the story—until now! This fantastic book pays [them] tribute…"
—*The Bloomsbury Review*

"A vibrant and multilayered picture of early
Alaskan and of American society in the 1890's"
—*School Library Journal* starred review

"A strong sense of a rugged era"
—*Publishers Weekly*

CHILDREN OF THE GOLD RUSH

ISBN 978-0-9627530-4-6, $15.95

**Willa Literary Award, Children's non-fiction,
Women Writing the West, 1999**

Individual stories, vintage photos, and historic memorabilia chronicle the
adventures of youngsters who came North with their parents in search of gold.

"This excellent, well-researched book offers a rare peek into
a fascinating culture, history, and people, in portraits of eight intrepid children."
—*Kirkus Reviews*